PENGUIN BOOKS

WHERE WILL YOU BE IN FIVE YEARS?

Arfeen Khan is a world-renowned speaker, strategist and consultant. For almost twenty years, he has helped over 2,00,000 people in thirty-four countries undergo personal and professional transformation. Khan has worked with an extensive range of people, including CEOs, students, Bollywood celebrities and industrialists.

WHERE WILL YOU BE IN FIVE YEARS?

DREAM

PLAN

ACHIEVE

ARFEEN KHAN

PENGUIN BOOKS

An imprint of Penguin Random House

PENGUIN BOOKS

USA | Canada | UK | Ireland | Australia
New Zealand | India | South Africa | China | Singapore

Penguin Books is part of the Penguin Random House group of companies
whose addresses can be found at global.penguinrandomhouse.com

Published by Penguin Random House India Pvt. Ltd
4th Floor, Capital Tower 1, MG Road,
Gurugram 122 002, Haryana, India

First published in Penguin Books by Penguin Random House India 2017

10 9 8 7 6 5 4 3 2

The views and opinions expressed in this book are the author's own and the
facts are as reported by him, which have been verified to the extent possible,
and the publishers are not in any way liable for the same.

ISBN 9780143425014

Typeset in Adobe Garamond Pro by Manipal Digital Systems, Manipal

Printed at Manipal Technologies Limited, India

www.penguin.co.in

This is a legitimate digitally printed version of the book and therefore might not
have certain extra finishing on the cover.

Contents

Contents

I

You Can Shape Your Life

'I believe that tomorrow is another day and I believe in miracles.'

— Audrey Hepburn

Y ou can shape your tomorrow, today, now, this very moment. It doesn't matter whether you believe in miracles or not. What matters is that you should believe in yourself and the power you have to make your future what you want it to be. *Today* is the most important day in your life. *Now* is the only moment over which you have control. This is what it means to live in the *present*. Being present in the moment and taking action is what really matters.

When we think of time, we think of it in terms of the past, the present and the future. There is in fact one more aspect of time and that is being absent. Your presence in the present is very important. If you are absent from your present, it will affect your future. A person becomes absent from his or her present when he or she dwells too much in the past or when they put off things till the future. You are absent from your present if you get impatient with where you are now, not focus on what's happening around you at this very moment, and want to get ahead to the future without experiencing the present.

Your Best Is Yet to Come

When the rest of your life lies ahead of you and you are optimistic about the future, you want your life to happen as soon as possible. On the other hand, there's a wise bit of advice to consider, which goes something like this: 'Live today as if it were your last.'

Now, imagine that you have a job interview scheduled for tomorrow. If you think today is the last day of your life, you will probably not care for the interview or prepare for it. That's not the right attitude to have. Especially when you have to prepare for something important that will shape your future. So, the ideal thing is to do what you can and should do at the moment. Do not get into the 'let me do that tomorrow' frame of mind as that is procrastination. Nor should you have an 'I don't care for the future because I live for the moment' attitude and not plan for what lies ahead. **Do you want to make decisions, do you want to know how you can take action right now? You can access the online course, 'Where Will You Be in Five Years', worth Rs 13,000 on www.wherewillyoubein5years.com to start taking charge of your life.**

Live in the moment but be aware of the past and hopeful about the future. When divers stand on a diving board, they are focused on the dive that they are about to take. At the same time, they think about all that they have learnt from their previous dives. You may call it experience or wisdom. They also know that they want to give it their best shot. Yet they know that in the future they'll dive better than this.

It is the same with people from any profession—dancers, singers, painters, writers, runners, salespersons or even people working in a café. If they believe in progressively getting better and better, they know that the performance they are about to give, the song they are about to sing, the art they are about to create, the race they are about to run, the deal they are about to close or the coffee they are about to brew could be their best, their masterpiece, but only for now, for this moment in time. In the future, there will be opportunities to do something even better, but that's for later. As they say in the locker room, 'You are only as good as the last game you played, but don't you want to be better than this in the next game you will play?'

You can take action right now, at this very moment, and this will definitely influence your future. If you plant a seed now and nurture it, it will grow into something that will provide shade and bear fruit in the future. If you start your journey now, you will reach your destination sooner than if you were to start it tomorrow. But you can't hurry the process or get impatient.

Be Calm and Stay Focused

It's your choice: you can stay where you are and ignore the opportunities that come your way. A wise man once said that in the future you will only regret what you did not do, not what you did. So, act now. Your actions have consequences, and your future is a result of your actions. You swing a bat with the intention of making contact with the ball and hitting it home or over the boundary. Whether you hit the ball or not comes later. What matters now is that you swing the bat to hit. If you have practised your swing and your attention is focused on the ball, then, you are more likely to hit it than to miss it.

Once you understand why something happens, you can learn how to make it happen, and then, you can make it happen again and again. Events don't occur without a reason. When you see a rainbow, you know that it's not a miracle or a mystery. It's a phenomenon. Once you understand the process by which a rainbow is formed, you can recreate the same effect. You don't have to wait for a rainy day; you can recreate the seven colours of the rainbow by playing around with light and pieces of lens or glass.

Learn the Formula for Success

What emotions do you experience when you see people who you think are healthier, happier, stronger, wealthier or more successful than you are? Do you envy them and wonder how they became who they are? Do you think they just got lucky or that the stars were in their favour? Or do you do something about it? Do you try to find out how they got to where they are? Have you considered the possibility that if they could do or achieve something, so can you? Instead of envying someone, have you thought about emulating them?

What if I told you that there is a formula for achieving anything you want, whether it is professional and financial success, or stability in your love life. I understand you might find this hard to believe. It's natural to be sceptical because the term 'formula' is generally associated with something that is too easy and therefore not reliable or trustworthy, like a 'quick fix'. However, let me explain what I mean by a formula for success. There are two types of formulas—magic and rational. The magic formula is abracadabra, hocus-pocus, etc. You don't know how it works, why it works or even if works. It's something that is beyond understanding. You chant a mantra or perform an action and things are supposed to happen.

On the surface, the rational formula may sound similar and simple. You perform a set of actions and get a result. However, the rational formula differs from the magic formula in one important aspect. It can be demonstrated, like a mathematical formula and you can understand how it works. There is a plausible explanation for why it works. It has been proved that when you put certain elements together in a certain order or manner or perform certain actions in a specific sequence, you will get a certain result or a set of results. The earlier example of creating a rainbow by refracting light through a glass prism is just that. You are applying a formula with which you are able to recreate what happens in nature when it rains, and after which the sun shines.

The key lies in the knowledge that white light is made up of seven colours. When white light passes through a glass prism or raindrops, it splits or is refracted and you get the seven colours of the rainbow. Is this a trick or an illusion? It depends on how you look at it. When seen with the knowledge of the principles of light refraction, it makes sense. In the absence of this knowledge, it can appear illusory or magical.

Similarly, when you view a successful person with envy, you see only the result and not the reason. On the other hand, when you analyse and understand how someone achieved this success, you realize it is possible to replicate the same result with a series of carefully performed actions. Just like in a mathematical or chemical formula: if you use the right elements and make the right calculations, you will get the right results. Once you understand this basic rational formula, you will know that there is a law that governs success. Successful people know and understand this law and use it to their advantage.

It is also important to understand that there are smart and systematic ways of doing things and there are also random and haphazard ways. This is what sets the successful apart from the rest. This is what differentiates a person who possesses knowledge or wisdom and has the wherewithal to apply it to achieve success.

Are You Denying Yourself a Shot at Success?

We often hear people talking about someone who is extremely talented or gifted. They talk about talent as if it were a rare thing, a miracle or a magic formula. It is not. Success isn't merely the result of being 'born with a talent' or with a 'god-given gift'. It is the outcome of a series of calculated and deliberate actions taken by the so-called talented or gifted person.

A successful sportsperson may be inherently talented, but if he or she does not convert this talent into action and apply it by practising in a systematic manner, then, no amount of talent will help. It is as if the talent did not exist. If they don't activate their talent and abilities through regular practice and become champions, then, they will remain regular players. This is the case with any successful person, be it an artist, an actor, a singer, a musician, a salesperson, a doctor, an engineer, a writer, a gardener, a farmer or a mountain climber.

Now let's ask the most important question: Are you moving towards success or away from it? A mountain climber is not a climber when he/she is at the base of the mountain. He/she won't get any closer to the summit by circling around the base of the mountain or walking away from it. The climber becomes a climber when he/she is on his/her way, attempting to climb, making the journey towards the summit.

What is your journey? Do you know your summit or your destination? Do you know the mountains you wish to climb?

Do you have a plan? Do you have a roadmap to guide you? Do you know someone who has climbed the mountain before you?

Would You Cross a Road Blindfolded?

Would you sign a document without reading it? Would you be able to give an answer if you didn't understand the question? Then, how do you expect to get where you want to be in your life if you don't have a clear vision or a focused plan. Even if you do have a plan, are you taking the right steps to get to your destination? How can you expect your dreams to be fulfilled if you don't do anything about them? Understand this: there are some things which you can change and there are some things which you can't.

Therefore, focus on the things that are within your *sphere of influence* and the ones you can modify or change to your advantage. You can't make it rain. So, if you want the plants in your garden to grow, you need to water them. You can't see in the dark; so you need a flashlight. You can choose to ignore your talents and gifts. You can choose to envy others who are happier, healthier or more successful than you are and say that they got better breaks or were born with many advantages. This is not very different from waiting for it to rain or peering into the darkness without a flashlight.

On the other hand, if you want to, you can discover your potential for success and use this potential to make your life fulfilling.

This book can become the instrument that will change your life for the better. It's not going to happen overnight. Sorry to disappoint you if that's what you wanted to hear.

Good Things Take Time to Happen

However, you don't have to wait longer than is necessary for them to happen. There is a way through which you can make great things happen in your life. All you need to do is learn the formulas for success. They are not difficult and may even seem simple and easy once you learn and start using them. They are nothing but tried and tested methods that successful people have applied to achieve what they wanted, again and again.

Something Is Impossible Only If You Think It Is

This book contains wisdom that I have gleaned by studying the lives of many successful people. I do not say that everything that you will read in this book is new or even groundbreaking. On the contrary, most of the formulas that I have listed in this book are not really secrets. They will appear to be extremely simple and easy. They are like the 'egg of Columbus'.

When Christopher Columbus announced his intention to go on a voyage to discover a route to the new world, people told him it was impossible. They said that the voyage of discovery on which he was embarking was not only foolhardy but doomed to fail.

In response, Columbus challenged his critics to balance an egg on its tip on a table. When they said it was impossible, Columbus put some salt on the table and demonstrated how easily the egg could be balanced on its tip if placed in the salt. Of course, this is an apocryphal story and historians say that there is no record to show that Columbus actually balanced the egg to silence his critics. However, the story, true or not, tells you how easy it is to give up on something even before trying it. Also, the fact that you cannot balance an egg on its tip but you can do so by putting salt on the table proves that what might, in hindsight, seem obvious or even easy is not always so, especially if you have a negative or a defeatist approach.

Columbus was just another sailor before he discovered America. All successful people have led ordinary lives before they achieved exceptional levels of success because they were willing to go to extraordinary lengths to learn how to attract and achieve success, abundance, happiness, strength and the support of the people around them.

They knew something which most of us don't. *They knew that, despite what everyone else says or feels, there is always a way.* Once you put your mind to it, there is no obstacle that cannot be overcome, no sea that cannot be crossed, no mountain that cannot be climbed, and no problem that cannot be solved. If your will is strong enough and you are willing to use your mind to look for a way and find it, you will succeed. **Your mindset plays an important role in whatever you do; to know how to have the right mindset, log on to www.wherewillyoubein5years.com to access the free online course, 'Where Will You Be in Five Years'.** Once you know this, you can make things happen the way you want them to. It's as simple as that.

Begin with Your Mind

It doesn't matter if the success that you see around you, which someone else has achieved, appears at first to be nothing short of a miracle. What matters is what you think.

Now, the following questions may seem very simple. They aren't.

- Do you think you have an open mind?
- Do you think you too can become successful, rich and happy?
- Are you strong and intelligent enough to believe that your mind can absorb and accept some concepts that may seem alien to you at first? Are you willing to start your journey towards success by first beginning it in your mind?

I have seen the awe in people's eyes when they realize that the seeds of success lie within us, in our own mind, and not in something that is beyond our control, such as fate or fortune.

I am going to forget modesty for a moment and tell you the truth about what I do. As a performance coach and motivational speaker, I help other people transform their lives for the better. Most people believe that what I do is almost as amazing as a miracle. I meet hundreds of people during my seminars. At every seminar, large numbers of people come up to me to discuss their financial problems, expecting an instant solution. There are no magic formulas involved in my interactions with people. But, as I said earlier, there are real formulas, just like in mathematics. It's just a matter of keeping an open mind and learning these formulas.

Though I admit that I help and influence people, what I essentially do is enable a person to discover within him/her the seeds of success. Hence, the most rewarding aspect of what I do is to witness people, who previously seemed resigned to their fate, transform themselves and become active agents of their future, defining and creating their own success.

In my interactions, I use my knowledge and experience to activate the energy lying dormant within a person by acting as a catalyst. I have written this book with the intention that it will act as a catalyst and ignite that spark within you.

You can be where you want to be in five years, if you know where you want to be, why you want to be there, and how you can get there. You can get there if you take action today. However, in order to get there, you need to know what you want.

Learn How to Differentiate between Living and Making a Living

We desire many things: a career, friends, time, wealth, a house, a car, opportunities to meet people, see places . . . the list goes on. Is that all there is to life? Wanting and achieving what we want? This is one of the mistakes most of us make when we think of our goals. We think that our wants and goals are the same. This is the same mistake many of us made when we were very young and were asked what we wanted to become when we grew up. Isn't this what you said? I want to be an actor or a singer or a football player or a doctor or an engineer, and so on. You replied, keeping in mind a career instead of a life that would be fulfilling in all possible ways. You were thinking of how to 'make' a living rather than actually 'living'.

It's all right because most of us didn't know any better when we were young except perhaps John Lennon. Apparently he said that he wanted to be happy when he grew up. Don't we all want to be? Happy, I mean.

I am going to tell you a very important truth. Your happiness does not depend on your career choice. Your success too has nothing to do with what you do for a living. True happiness and success come from how you do what you do and why you do it.

Plan and Prepare Now for the Future You Want

The motivation to become a plumber or a pianist cannot be the same. It cannot be just to earn a living. The passion to do great things does not come from the rewards it will bring, be it wealth or fame. Passion goes deeper and it is what this book will explore.

Finally—Let Go of the Fear of Failure

The future is the place or destination you have to reach. Your life is the journey. Every phase in your life represents a stage of progress towards this place or destination. During this journey, your choices can change. Your desires can evolve. However, some of your goals will have to remain steady. Otherwise, you will fritter away your focus, your strength and your efforts in meaningless pursuits.

Now, let us focus on some important questions: Do you know what your beliefs, strengths and goals are? Do you know what you are willing to do to remain true to them? Do you know what obstacles you need to overcome in order to achieve success?

You don't have to predict the future. You only need to prepare for it. *What you do now, will define your tomorrow.*

Between taking off and becoming airborne, the pilot of an aircraft handles many functions while taking into account multiple factors such as speed, inclination, weather, resistance, visibility, etc. Similarly, between kicking the ball and scoring a goal, a football or soccer player coordinates his aim, pace and the force with which he or she sends the ball hurtling towards the goal. An actor takes a deep breath, calms the mind and the nerves, visualizes his/her performance, and experiences the audience's applause even before it happens. Preparing for your life begins here and now. You can foresee your future based on your thoughts and the actions you will take today.

Passion is important, but another key ingredient to succeed in life is persistence. If you are committed to your goals, then, you will persevere with your efforts until you are ready. As Bruce Lee once said, 'I am not afraid of a person who knows 10,000 different ways to kick. I am afraid of the person who knows one kick but has practised it 10,000 times.'

Failure is afraid of the person who knows the formula for success and is willing to apply it. Failure will run away from the person who is not afraid of failing. You don't have to be a genius to figure this out. People who are healthier, happier, wealthier, more popular or successful actually do things in a different way from the rest. That is why they succeed where others fail.

Which of These Questions Do You Usually Ask Yourself?

Is it, what does the future have in store for me? Or is it, how can I make my own future and get what I want?

If you are the kind of person who is willing to ask the second question, then congratulations; you have taken the first step towards a great future. Stop waiting for great things to happen. Start making them happen.

2

Why Five Years?

'Five years from now, you're the same person except for the people you've met and the books you've read.'

— John Wooden

Consider this: Most educational programmes or courses require between three and five years of continuous study by a student to obtain a degree. Similarly, in most democratic countries, the term of an elected head is generally between four and five years. Also, many countries implement five-year plans to achieve a particular goal. Even human resource professionals are of the opinion that an employee who doesn't stay in a job or with a company for at least three to five years might not be a reliable candidate. It has hence been observed that real and substantial changes or milestones of growth or development occur in five-year stages. This is evident in every sphere of life.

Organic or sustainable growth takes time. You can make small changes in a month or over a few months, but to achieve real and long-lasting transformation you need to plan, prepare and persevere for at least five years. Why five years? Why not three years?

There is nothing wrong in making a three-year plan, but it might be too short a time to achieve something substantial. Of course, you can plan for the next year or even the next month, but to make a big change in your life, it makes sense to plan for at least five years from now. Great things take time to plan and build, whether it is a career, a company or a relationship.

Also, five years give you ample room to realistically plan, prepare, modify and achieve what you want. You might achieve what you originally planned to do in five years within three years and that is good. On the other hand, it's possible that you might end up stretching your three-year plan into a five-year plan. When this happens, the sense of achievement is tinged with a sense of delay and disappointment, and this can affect your future plans.

Not Too Early, Not Too Late

There are many examples in the business industry where organizations or companies have projected plans for shorter periods and failed to accomplish them. Despite the emphasis on quarterly or annual growth in boardrooms, many companies take at least five years to become successful.

It was anything but a case of overnight success for the delivery company, FedEx. Even though it opened its doors to business in 1971, Federal Express turned profitable only in 1975, almost five years later. Today, the company is a leader in its category. Hence, it is an established fact that achievements which are significant and which last long also take a significant amount of time to achieve.

Did you know that the hugely successful animation movie *Toy Story* took over five years to make? The idea for *Toy Story*, which was released in 1995, was sown way back in 1988 when Pixar movies produced a short film called *Tin Toy*. The sequel to the first *Toy Story* was released almost four years later, in 1999. Imagine if the makers of *Toy Story* had been in a hurry. Do you think it would have marked a watershed in the history of animated movies? Probably not. Turning points in a person's life, in a relationship or in the growth of a company, occur every five years or so.

It's been proved that the five-year period is a practical time frame for realistically achieving a goal. So, why not ten years? A lot can happen in ten years, including changes which might drastically affect your plans as well as your life. What really matters is what happens in the first five years. It breaks down the length of time into something about which you can feel good in the short term. You can also think of a ten-year plan as two five-year plans to make it more achievable.

Then again, three, five or ten are just arbitrary numbers. You, and only you, can and should decide for yourself whether your goals are achievable in three years or whether they need ten years or whether you can complete them in five years. After all, it's three, five or ten years of your life. It's up to you.

Is the Long Run a Slow Run or a Steady Run?

I know a friend who ran the London Marathon last year. If you had seen her five or six years ago, you would have laughed if she had told you that she was going to run a marathon. In fact, some people did laugh at Geeta when she started running. At 175 pounds (eighty kilograms), she was huffing and puffing after running just 500 metres. Her lack of fitness did not make a pretty sight.

Never a sporty or athletic person, she was in her late thirties when she decided to do something about her weight, her health and her life. Guess how long it took Geeta to run her first marathon? Naturally, Geeta did not run a marathon in the first year. She took part in a five-kilometre run after training for a year. The next year, she took part in a ten-kilometre run, and the year after she ran a half-marathon (twenty-one kilometres).

Almost four years after she took up running regularly, she thought she was ready to run her first marathon. Did she succeed? It depends on how you measure success. Geeta ran for about thirty kilometres, but for the next twelve kilometres to the finishing line, she limped, hobbled and walked. That's right. She made it to the finishing line but she was not completely ready. Did she fail? No, she didn't. She analysed her training regimen and her diet. She made some changes, and the following year, again participated in the marathon. She later told me what she felt as she crossed the finishing line. She said, 'I didn't feel exhausted. I felt exhilarated. I felt like I could run a few more miles.'

Today, Geeta runs an average of six kilometres every day, and she clocks enough miles every week to equal a marathon. She intends to participate in at least one marathon every year. Running no longer feels like a chore or a compulsion; it has become a happy ritual, almost second nature to her. Do you see the transformation that took place in Geeta's life? She lost weight, regained her health, became a more active, healthier and happier person. But most of all, she adopted a habit that had the potential to stay with her all her life.

To Stay Steady, Find the Balance

There are two key takeaway lessons that I wish to point out in this story. The first one is that Geeta made a lifestyle change. From a sedentary lifestyle, she moved on to an active one. Just as you brush your teeth every day, Geeta runs six kilometres every day. Running has become a habit, an everyday ritual for her. Now, imagine if she had tried to do something as drastic as run a marathon within a year or two of training. She would have failed as she did when she attempted her first marathon in the fourth year. The failure would have been more devastating, and she probably wouldn't have bounced back. She probably would have given up running altogether if she had attempted too much, too soon.

The second lesson is that Geeta struck a balance. Do you know how much weight Geeta lost over a period of five years? She dropped more than twenty-two kilograms or almost fifty pounds. Today, Geeta weighs fifty-nine kilograms or about 130 pounds. However, her weight only tells a part of the story. The real story is that she achieved all this by not going on a crash diet or an exercise regimen that she hated.

When I told Geeta what an extraordinary achievement it was, she shrugged her shoulders and said nonchalantly, 'I was eating more calories than I was burning. It didn't make sense. There was no balance between input and output. The more calories I consumed, the more exercise I needed to do to burn them. If I became more active, I needed enough calories to energize my actions. Once I realized this, it was not at all complicated. I just had to restore the balance.'

A crash diet or an exercise regimen might help you to lose weight but would you be able to stay that way? Unlike many people who lose weight and then put it on again, Geeta has maintained her weight at 58–59 kilograms for more than a year.

That's because she has understood the importance of a lifestyle change and of maintaining a balance. We will examine these two important concepts in detail in our next chapter.

3

The Basics of a Lifestyle Design

'All I am offering is the truth. Nothing more.'

— Morpheus, in *The Matrix*

A sandwich or a salad? Gym or Pilates? Glasses or contact lenses? A paperback or an e-book? A phone call or an e-mail? An employee or an entrepreneur? A cup of tea or coffee, or a glass of milk? The lift or the staircase? The city or the countryside? A seaside resort or a forest hideaway?

Whether it is what you eat for breakfast, or how you wish to exercise, communicate or read, what you wish do for a living, how you travel, how or where you wish to spend your holiday, you always have a choice. Your choices define who you are and your life. Don't they?

Your career, friends, life partner; what you wear, what you do to relax—these are all conscious and deliberate choices that you make. Your philosophy or world view, your thoughts and beliefs about money, society and culture—they shape your personality and form a part of your lifestyle.

Now think: Is your personality a product of your external environment and influences or a manifestation of your inner beliefs? Are you living a life that is expected of you by your friends, family members, colleagues and the community in which you live? Or are you living the life you want to live?

When you make a choice, it is often influenced by many external factors and influences. These include other people's opinions, a collection of your past experiences and your hopes for the future, and perhaps even your fears and worries.

When you want to eat a piece of cake, you are tempted by its visual appearance and also because you remember how good it tasted the last time you had it. At the same time, you are worried about the number of calories it contains, and start planning the amount of exercise you would have to do the next morning in order to compensate for your present indulgence. You almost say 'no'. Then, you see your friend put a spoonful in her mouth. You watch the ecstatic way in which she savours the mouthful. You are swayed and you give in, you indulge. Did you make the decision to eat the cake or did your friend influence your decision? There are many people who find faults with their situation and try to blame it on others. There are very few people who are willing to own up and take responsibility for who they are, what they do and why they do it.

What Is Your Truth?

Don't be bewildered by the tone of the question. It is, no doubt, philosophical but it is not as difficult a question as it might seem at first. Nor is it as easy as you think it is. If the question makes you uncomfortable, don't worry. That's exactly what it is supposed to do. However, the best part is that you are not answerable to anyone but yourself. Nobody but you will know whether you chose the red or the blue pill. Nobody but you will know whether you are living the life that you desire or a life of illusion, a life that is expected of you by others.

Now think, what if Sachin Tendulkar had gone to medical school? What if Richard Branson had chosen a nine-to-five job? What if J.K. Rowling had found gainful employment as a secretary and had written official communication letters instead of fantasy novels? Why would you or anyone else know or care about a schoolteacher named Gordon Matthew Thomas Sumner? He became famous as Sting, the musician. Imagine if he had continued teaching mathematics! Do you find it hard to believe that Michael Jordan did not make it to the varsity basketball team because he was considered too short? If he had taken that rejection to heart, the world would have lost the opportunity of watching the greatest basketball player of all time in action.

After going through so many examples, it's time to ask a difficult question. Is your life a lie? Have you created a fake personality based on what other people want you to be? What if you were to stop doing what everyone else wants you to do and started doing what you want to do? Would you find your life more fulfilling? Would you be happier? It's time to seek answers to the most important question: What is your truth? It's never too late to ask yourself this question. You have the rest of your life to find the answers.

Why Wait a Lifetime?

Four friends met at a college reunion after more than two decades. One was a rich and successful investment banker; another was an entrepreneur and industrialist; the third one was a senior officer in the armed forces; and the fourth one claimed that he had already taken retirement. However, they suspected that he was unemployed. They were all in their forties. So naturally, the attention of the three, who were doing well in their respective fields, was on the person who claimed to be living a retired life.

At first, they felt sorry for him and asked him what his interests and professional background were, so they could help him find a job. However, when Sameer insisted that he was actually retired and was not looking for any kind of employment, the pity they had felt just a few moments earlier suddenly turned into envy. They couldn't imagine how anyone could afford to retire so early in his life. They were curious to know how he had made his fortune. Had he made a killing on the stock market? Had he inherited money? Had he won a lottery? Had he married someone rich? He shook his head and said, 'It's nothing like what you think. I didn't make a fortune. I just made a few smart choices.' His friends didn't understand. Did he have a million bucks in the bank? No, he didn't. Did he play golf? No. Did he visit the casino or go on a holiday every other week? No. Then, what was the point of being retired? Didn't he get bored? How did he spend all his time?

'I spend a lot of time reading and thinking about what I read,' said Sameer. 'I also meet a lot of people, friends who are smarter than I am, and I find it interesting to talk to them. I do a bit of woodwork and carpentry, make furniture, and spend some time in the garden, growing vegetables in the backyard. I go for long walks with my dog and teenaged daughter.'

Sameer saw a uniform look of disbelief on the faces of his three friends. He shrugged and continued, 'Once in a while, I travel with my family. We make it a point to visit new places. Next month, we are going to Kenya and Tanzania.

My daughter has always wanted to witness the great African wildebeest migration in the Maasai Mara National Reserve. So, we are doing that.'

His three friends were dumbstruck. They realized that though Sameer was not very rich, he had enough to take care of his family and their needs. He didn't have an exciting career, but he didn't seem to mind it one bit.

'I also play in a local band. If you ever come to my town, visit The Narrow Lane. It's a very popular pub. Our band plays most Wednesdays and Fridays, 7 p.m. onwards.' His friends started laughing. 'But you are tone-deaf. You can't even tell the difference between two different tunes,' one of his friends said. That was indeed true. When they were in college, the other three friends had formed a band and used to play music at local events. Sameer was their friend, but he was not a part of the band because he could not contribute musically.

'I still miss a few notes while we play, but nobody cares, especially the other band members. As for the audience, they are not the fussiest critics,' said Sameer. 'It's just a group of friends having fun. It's not like we are giving a performance.'

Who Decides What You Do and When?

While his friends had focused on their careers, Sameer had chosen to retire. He'd created a life for himself and his family that was not typical. People generally retire when they are sixty years old. Until then they are expected to pursue a career or at least be gainfully employed.

What made Sameer choose retirement in his forties? Perhaps he had made enough money and did not want to work so hard for the rest of his life. However, this might not be a plausible explanation because his friends were definitely wealthier than him. Then, why were they still working? Perhaps Sameer had lost his job and couldn't find another. Or, tired of the rat race, he had quit. We don't know. We can only speculate but, in such cases, we usually tend to come to the conclusion that there might be something wrong with the person or that something went wrong in his life. Why?

Who says you can retire only at a particular age? There are people who continue to work even in their seventies. On the other hand, there are people like Sameer who choose to retire early in life. Who says you should take only one vacation every year? There are people who can afford to take more than one. There are others who prefer not to take even one. Who says you shouldn't take a nap in the daytime or make love in the afternoon? Would it make you feel guilty if you did? Why do you eat popcorn when you watch a movie? Why do you read a newspaper while you have your breakfast? Why do you wear sober-coloured trousers to work and not something bright? Why do most men cut their hair short while most women wear theirs long? Why do we do everything according to a pattern? We do what we do (or at least most of it) because we don't want to upset the proverbial applecart. There are laws and rules and there are conventions. Some rules are made for a reason. If you are a smoker, you are not supposed to smoke in a public place. You are also not supposed to urinate in a public place. If you break these rules, you could be reprimanded, fined or even arrested. You stop at red lights while driving. While using a pedestrian crossing, you look in both directions to ensure your safety. If you don't follow these rules, you could hurt yourself or someone else, or even kill someone or get killed. You say hello when you pick up the phone. You return the greeting when someone wishes you 'good day'. If you don't, you are being rude and could upset that person. Do you see the pattern? Some of these are rules; not following them can cause discomfort to others, get you into trouble or even cause accidents. Some are matters of etiquette which may not cause as much damage if you don't follow them but can still be frowned upon. You need to follow rules and laws but you need not always conform to conventions or patterns. Just because everyone wears a white shirt doesn't mean you too have to. Just because everyone wears high heels doesn't mean you too have to. Just because everyone looks for a job after they graduate doesn't mean you have to. You could start your own company and be an entrepreneur. Or you could take a year off and travel around the world. Just because all managers in a company are of a mature age, it doesn't mean a young person can't become a manager. You don't have to be part of the herd. You can lead the herd or you can be on your own. It's up to you.

The herd mentality settles in when there are no original thoughts in the mind, when there is no will to try something new, when the mind is closed because of the fear of failure. Would you want to live your life worrying about what would happen if you did what you wanted to do instead of what everyone else was doing? Would you do what someone else wanted you to do, or what others expected you to do? **Your identity controls everything you think, every emotion you experience and every action you take. I suggest you take advantage of my free training course 'Where Will You Be in Five Years' on www.wherewillyoubein5years.com.**

How the Way We Work Has Changed and Why?

In recent years, our work pattern has witnessed a major paradigm shift. The information age ushered in a new breed of workforce called knowledge workers. Companies realized that flexible working hours were not only possible but also highly productive.

Modern communication methods, such as e-mail, chat and videoconferencing, along with what became standard tools, such as mobile phones, laptops and other devices, enabled people to work seamlessly even when they were not physically present in the same office. In fact, people who lived in different geographical locations and even in different time zones could share information, collaborate and work together by using online work platforms. Technological innovations have changed the way we work. The nine-to-five schedule is no longer necessary. In fact, what was once a convenience has now become a potential obstacle to productivity. Concepts like working from home and telecommuting have become popular.

You might be thinking, what does this have to do with me? For that matter, what does this have to do with anything? Well, how you work and how you live your life are intrinsically linked, isn't it? You cannot deny the fact that your work forms a big part of your life. Now, whoever said, 'Choose a job you love and you will never have to work another day in your life', probably did not understand the importance of work and what it really meant. Work is work, whether you enjoy it or not.

Work Isn't Life and Life Isn't Work

Why else would we talk about a work–life balance? In the corporate world, though the discussion and debate on work–life balance has been going on for long, it has never been more achievable than it is today. In his book, *The 4-Hour Workweek: Escape the 9–5, Live Anywhere and Join the New Rich*, Timothy Ferriss hit the 'work–life balance' nail on the head. He busted some long-standing beliefs and myths. Instead of working long and hard, he showed how people could work just four hours a week and still make enough money to enjoy doing what they liked the rest of the time.

The adage, 'Work smart not hard', has been going around for years. Ferriss demonstrated how you could, why you should, and the rewards for doing so. Leisure was no longer reserved for the privileged or the lazy. It was an achievable and even admirable goal. Lifestyle design as a concept soon took off as more and more people realized that you didn't have to work longer hours or till you were sixty. You could retire in your forties, if that's what you wanted to do.

You could design the life you wanted.

What Is a Lifestyle Design?

When you move into a house, you want to make it cosy and comfortable. You want the place to be a reflection of your personality. So you furnish it accordingly. You define your space by surrounding yourself with things or possessions that make you feel at home. What you are essentially doing is designing your home to suit your taste. Of course, you may consult with or hire an interior designer to advise you, but you are the one who makes the choices. Similarly, there are specific aspects in life to which we need to attend and make our choices accordingly. Education is one such thing. Career, another.

This brings us to another aspect, money. We need money to live. It's not just about putting bread on the table, is it? We need money to buy things like clothes, a house, furniture, a car, appliances, electronic goods, and for entertainment, like going on a vacation or eating out.

Another important point to consider is time. You know that your time is limited. We all have a finite number of years, and therefore it is important to prioritize and allocate enough time to each aspect of life. To put it in a nutshell, lifestyle design is about putting these choices together. You choose what to do and when to do it. You just need to know how to attend to the most important things, the things that really matter, and avoid what's irrelevant and inconsequential. Once you figure that out, you can design a lifestyle that fits your dreams and aspirations.

At this stage you need to take a good look at the 'wheel of life'.

Let's Take the Wheel of Life for a Spin

The 'wheel of life' is a simple and handy tool that enables you to examine the important aspects of your life. It gives you the perspective you need to look at your life in a holistic manner, so that you can identify the parts of your life you might be neglecting or the ones that need more attention.

Imagine that you are walking a tightrope. If someone shouts or makes a noise, you lose your balance. Why? You get distracted. If you are really focused, then, you won't allow any distractions to enter your consciousness.

If you are driving a vehicle at high speed, there are more chances of your losing control while taking a turn. When you are busy with your life, working hard, working long hours, making money, spending money, spending time, buying things, meeting people and so on, it's possible to lose your perspective. When you lose your perspective, you also lose your balance.

The wheel of life puts your life into perspective and restores the balance.

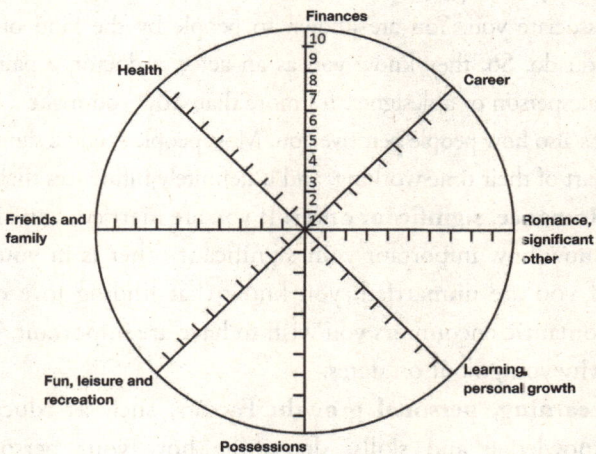

Look at the different aspects mentioned in the wheel of life. Let's examine each aspect, see what it constitutes and how it contributes towards making your life more fulfilling and meaningful.

1. **Health:** You cannot deny the importance of maintaining your health and fitness levels. It influences your ability to work and also your ability to enjoy life. What you eat, the nutritional value of the food, how or how much you exercise, the kind of activities you have in your daily routine, your lifestyle, they all influence your health.

2. **Finances:** Your financial situation or how much money you earn defines the kind of lifestyle you can afford. You need money

for not only the essential things in life like food, clothes, a house and travel but also for possible eventualities like medicines and health care, or educational expenses to improve your skills.

3. **Career:** Your professional life defines you. Not only do you earn money through it, but it is also the label with which people associate you. You are known to people by the kind of work you do. So, they know you as an actor, a doctor, a painter, a salesperson or a designer. It's more than how you make a living; it's also how people perceive you. Most people spend a significant part of their time working, and it definitely influences their life.

4. **Romance, significant other:** If you are married, you already know how important your significant other is in your life. If you are unmarried, you know that finding love or the romantic encounters you wish to have are important. That's why you go out on dates.

5. **Learning, personal growth:** Factors, such as education, knowledge and skills, determine how your personality develops. As you grow older, you are expected to become wiser. If you don't update your knowledge or your skills, you can lose out on many opportunities in life.

6. **Possessions:** Your house, the stuff in your house, the clothes you wear, the car you drive, the PC or laptop or phone you use, they all determine how efficiently you perform your daily tasks. Your possessions create the environment in which you live. If you live in a noisy or unsafe environment, it affects your personality. If you are calm and collected, it is because of the immediate environment that your possessions have created around you.

7. **Fun, leisure and recreation:** All work and no play, as the saying goes, can make a person dull and turn him/her into a

bore. You need to allocate enough time to have some fun and indulge in your favourite leisure activities. If you are so busy that you don't have time to go on a holiday or spend time doing what refreshes you, you really need to rethink your priorities.

8. **Friends and family:** Our social interactions give our life its many flavours. If you are living with people with whom you have no emotional attachment, then you are neglecting an important aspect of your life which nurtures your zest and enthusiasm. After all, we are influenced by the company we keep. Negative people affect your life. **To learn how to deal with negative people around you, check out my free online course on www.wherewillyoubein5years.com.** Successful people always have the support and encouragement of family and friends. Behind every successful person, there is a group of people whose love and care provide the indispensable encouragement that is required for achieving success.

Balance the Wheel of Your Life

You may have noticed a scale numbered from one to ten on the wheel of life. This is to help you measure how satisfied you are with the different aspects of life. **You can do this exercise on www.wherewillyoubein5years.com/wheel to measure the different aspects of your life.** Ask yourself this: On a scale of one to ten, how satisfied am I with my health, finances and so on? You may feel healthy, but it's important to ask yourself whether you are eating the right kind of food, or whether you are getting enough physical exercise. If you think there is room for improvement, then, put a mark on the scale based on how much more you need to improve.

Ask yourself similar questions in terms of your financial situation. Are you earning as much as you think you should. Are you able to save enough? Do you have a diverse portfolio of investments that provide a reliable rate of return?

Do you remember the question I had asked you earlier in this chapter? What is your truth? Realizing how balanced your life is after marking your level of satisfaction on the wheel of life for each aspect is your moment of truth. Nobody but you needs to know your truth. However, the key is to be honest with yourself.

Does your wheel of life resemble something like this after you have marked it?

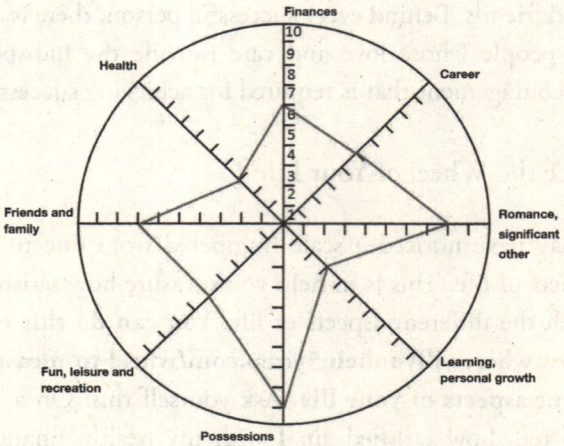

Don't worry. Nobody's perfect and nor is anybody's life. The important thing is to understand this: Simply by analysing each aspect of your life and marking the status on the wheel, you have taken the first step towards improving your life. Now you can plan how to improve the low points (those closer to the centre of the wheel) so that they match the aspects which are closer to the periphery.

There's Always Room for Improvement

When we write down something or draw a diagram, it helps us understand the concept better. That's what the wheel of life does. It illustrates the importance of achieving balance across the different aspects of life.

Here's another fun way to look at your life. Take a glass jar. Now put lemons into it till there is no more space to fill. Is the jar full? Yes, it is, but it is filled with lemons. Is there something else you can put into it? Like what? Maybe sugar? Take some fine sugar and pour it into the jar till it reaches the brim. Is the jar full now? Yes, it is full of lemons and sugar, but is there room for something else? What? How about some water? Pour some water into the jar. You will see that it flows through the sugar and the lemons and finds its way even though we had thought the jar was full.

Your life is the jar. The lemons, the sugar and the water are like the different aspects that we saw on the wheel of life. You may think that you are so busy with work that you don't have time for leisure. You are mistaken. There is always room in your life for each important aspect. Look closely at your life and you will know what to improve. We'll look at how you can improve your life in a systematic manner in the next chapter.

4

Where Are You Now?

'You will never be happy if you continue to search for what happiness consists of. You will never live if you are looking for the meaning of life.'

— Albert Camus

Whenever I plan a trip, I make a packing list just to make sure that I don't forget anything. Here is what a typical packing list looks like:

1. Shirts
2. Trousers
3. Underwear
4. Shoes
5. Toiletries
6. Laptop and charger
7. Phone charger
8. Tickets
9. ID card/passport
10. Camera

Is this list complete? No, it isn't. For instance, it does not contain belts, ties, sunglasses or socks. So, I add them to the list. I go through the list a few more times to check whether I have missed anything and then add a few more items. Why do I do this? Why do I bother to make a list?

What if I just started packing things instead of making a list? Well, let's say, I put all my clothes, toiletries and electronics into a bag. I close the bag and then I wonder, 'Did I put my socks in the bag? Or did I put in two pairs of trousers or three?' There's only one way to find out. I have to open the bag and rummage through it and make a mess of it. Or, depending on whether I have the time or I am in a patient mood, I can take out everything, one by one, to look for the socks or check whether I have packed the right number of trousers.

Do You See the Point of Making a List?

People make lists all the time. When they are going to the supermarket, when they are sending out invitations for a party or when they are starting their day. They make a list of things to buy, a list of people to invite, a list of things to do, and so on.

You may have heard of the 'bucket list', a list of things a person wants to do before he or she dies or kicks the bucket, so to speak. Well, do you have one? Do you have a list of things that you want to do in your life or with your life? Congratulations if you do. Take it out and go through it.

If you haven't made a list or if you can't find the list which you made, then, now is a good time to make that list or refresh it or rewrite it. Start writing down the things you want to do. You are probably thinking that you don't have to make a list right now, right at this moment, just because I told you to. However, I assure you that you will find this exercise enjoyable, memorable and perhaps even fruitful. So, please, please humour me and pretend that you are back in school, sitting in a classroom, and your teacher has told you to make a list. You can't leave the classroom until you make that list. Even in my seminars I always make sure everyone gets a notepad and a pen, so that they can note down the important things because we tend to forget those details later. You don't have a notepad or a piece of paper? No problem, just turn to the next page of this book and you will find some blank space where you can write that list. You don't have a pen? No problem, take out your smartphone and start typing that list. Stop making excuses and start making a list. Please write down at least ten items in your list.

Here's a sample list, just to give you an idea. This is somebody else's list. You don't have to follow the pattern given below. Just write down ten or more things that you want to do in your life.

1. Start saving at least __ per cent of my earnings
2. Go to the gym at least five days a week
3. Quit my job and start a company
4. Climb Mount Everest
5. Learn how to write a code
6. Learn Spanish
7. Buy a house by the time I am __ years old
8. Bungee jump
9. Meet my idol, _____, in person
10. Go on a cruise with my sweetheart

You might find some of the things in the above list weird or even pointless. Doesn't matter. The point is that everyone's list is unique. Some things on your list might not make sense to other people. So it's pretty understandable if you wish to keep your list to yourself.

You can write down below the things you want to do or achieve before you die:

1. _____
2. _____
3. _____
4. _____
5. _____
6. _____
7. _____
8. _____
9. _____
10. _____

Now, put a bookmark on this page and close this book. Close your eyes, and try to do the following three things:

1. Try to recall all the items in the packing list I mentioned at the beginning of the chapter.
2. Try to recall all the items on the sample list that was mentioned.
3. Try to recall all the items on your list.

Here's how I guess you fared in your memory test. You were able to recall more items on your list than in the packing list or the sample list. How come? The first two lists are not relevant to you and they don't excite you because they have nothing to do with you. They are just some random lists by some random people, and your mind doesn't think they are important enough to be remembered or committed to memory. Your list, on the other hand, is something about which you are passionate. Therefore, you could remember all the items on the list easily. Or were you not able to recall all of them?

The human mind is very complex. Understanding how it works explains why you are able to recall certain things and why you are not able to recall others. In terms of memory retention and recall, a smaller list is easier to remember. Also, if a list has a pattern in which the items have been listed out in order of their importance rather than at random, then, it becomes easier for you to remember them.

Let's try to put this to test. Look at the list below:

1. Blue
2. Yellow
3. Red
4. Green
5. Indigo
6. Violet
7. Orange

You don't immediately realize that the list comprises the colours of a rainbow. However, the colours are listed out in a random or different order, other than the one with which you are familiar—VIBGYOR. Once you realize this, you know that you don't need to commit the list to memory because you already know what the seven colours of the rainbow are.

Now, if you are asked to recollect this list in the same order or sequence, you will find it difficult. Why? This is because you have been taught so since childhood, and your mind thinks that the order known as VIBGYOR follows the pattern of a rainbow but BYRGIVO doesn't. It doesn't make sense to you.

This is probably how we learn the rules of a language. We know that a sentence makes sense when it is in a particular order, which is subject–verb–object. So for instance, if someone told you 'John wrote this book', it would make sense to you. However, if you are told, 'John this book wrote', you immediately sense that the sentence is incorrect because it does not follow the structure with which you are familiar. Yet, this is how someone would say it in the Japanese language because it follows a subject–object–verb structure.

Therefore, when you make a list, it helps to have a sequence or to follow a pattern. For instance, in a packing list, you can put down the clothes first, the toiletries next and then the electronic items. If you are making a to-do list for the day, it helps to list three things or the most important tasks at the top followed by the others. Why? So, you will have the energy to do what's important and not waste time on stuff that you can perhaps do later. So, making a list is important, but how you make it is also equally important.

Why Write Down Things?

The problem with making mental notes is that the ink tends to fade. Unless you have a uniquely sharp photographic memory—which is a very rare gift—you will be able to recall only a few items from a list which contains thirty items. On the other hand, it's easy to recall items from a list which contains only three things. Why?

It is quite normal to miss out on a few items from your list when you try to recall them, even though you had written them just a few minutes earlier. That's because your mind can focus on only a few things at a time. Listing out ten or more items in your mind is not an easy task, nor is it practical. This is why we write down things—so that we don't forget them.

Unless you intend to do only three or five things in a day, or pack only two or three things in your bag, or buy only three items from the store, it is always better to make a list. One of the most important benefits of making a list is that it gives you clarity and focus.

You can make a mental list of ten things. However, it is not easy to list them in the order of importance or in the order in which you want to do them. If you write them down, it becomes easier to rearrange them in a different order or sequence or even replace one item with another.

When a waiter in a restaurant writes down your order, it gives you a sense of security. You are confident that he will convey to the kitchen exactly what you and your group have ordered. If he does not write down your order, the chances of bringing you something else or jumbling up your order are more likely.

One of the surest ways to know 'where you are now' is to make a list. When you see someone successful, you think it is so because he or she is smarter or cleverer than you. Though this is possible, it may not really be the truth in most cases. *A successful person need not be smarter or cleverer than the rest. He or she just has to be clearer*. Clarity of vision brings your ambitions and goals into focus, whereby you are in a much better position to achieve them. When it's foggy, it is dangerous to drive or fly an airplane simply because one cannot see where one is going. Similarly, when you are not clear about what you want, who you want to be, where you are now, and where you want to be in five years, it becomes potentially dangerous to attempt things which you have not completely comprehended.

Clear Your Mind

Take a look around you. Take in the sights and listen to the sounds. If you are sitting in a café, you will notice that most of the people around are engrossed in some activity or the other besides drinking coffee. They are probably having a conversation and taking sips of coffee in between. If they are alone, they are either talking on their phone, tapping on the keypad of their laptop or smartphone, reading a book, newspaper or magazine, or listening to music.

In other words, they are all plugged into some external stimuli, whether it is electronic or print media, or social interactions with other people, such as having a discussion. You will find very few people sitting alone and focusing on sipping their tea or coffee.

In some restaurants or cafés, you will also hear music playing in the background, merging into the hubbub. Sometimes, there is a large television on the wall tuned to a news or sports channel. So, you are constantly in touch with or tuned to external stimuli, sometimes willingly and at other times even without your consent. In such an environment, you don't get an opportunity to know your thoughts. This is the reason why some resorts don't allow guests to bring their phones, play loud music or even bring small children. Establishing peace and quiet in an environment requires some drastic measures. When was the last time you heard the sound of birds singing, unadulterated by the sounds of vehicles driving by or honking? Or listened to the waves crashing down on the sand without any music playing in the background? When was the last time you experienced absolute silence, the kind in which you can almost hear a pin drop? If your answer is never or so long ago that you can't even remember, then, it is time you tried meditation.

For those who have never tried meditation, even the idea of it might seem pointless. After all, what's the point of sitting with your eyes closed, trying to focus on nothing? Why do they ask you to turn off your phone when you go to a concert or watch a tennis match? It's because you don't want to distract the performers or the players. Turning off your phone or putting it on silent while attending an important meeting or an interview helps you focus. Similarly, have you ever thought of turning off everything around you to clear your mind? Meditation is nothing but clearing your mind. Have I made it sound very simple and easy? Meditation is not easy, nor is it difficult. Imagine a clear, placid lake. That's your mind when you meditate. However, you rarely see a placid lake. There are always ripples or waves. Those are your thoughts. Too many thoughts can cause turmoil in your mind, create confusion and prevent you from achieving clarity and focus. **Utilize this unique opportunity to understand how you can achieve clarity in your life with my 'Where Will You Be in Five Years' online course worth Rs 13,000, which is available for free along with this book on www.wherewillyoubein5years.com.**

Don't Think about the Red Car

So, how can we control our thoughts? Well, you cannot control your thoughts. Not if you don't understand how your mind works. Let's play a little game. Tell yourself not to think about a red car. Now close your eyes and try hard not to think about one. What happens? You think of nothing but a red car. It's inevitable. Why? You are trying to do something which you cannot and are not supposed to do. You are trying to control your mind. You cannot. You can only calm your mind. Now, close your eyes, and let your mind think of the red car. Let it think of the red car as long as it wants to. You will notice that your mind starts wandering after a while. Other thoughts float in and flow through your mind. Let them. Stay still and keep your eyes closed. After a while, you will realize that you are no longer thinking about the red car; even if you are, it does not bother you any more. You feel a sense of serenity and peace seeping into your mind.

In some Eastern traditions, there is a belief that each one of us is born with a finite number of breaths in our life. That is, you can breathe a specific zillion number of times but not more than that. So, if you can prolong each breath, that is, breathe in deeply and make each breath last longer, then, you will be able to live a longer life. There is no rational basis for this hypothesis, but when you look at how your breathing influences your thoughts and actions, you realize that there is something that connects your breathing to the quality of your life.

If you play a song too slow or too fast, you distort its rhythm. You can barely make out the notes or the lyrics. You definitely cannot enjoy it. Now, notice the pattern of your breathing. Your breathing has a natural rhythm; once you find it and realize what it is, you will be able to understand why you are asked to focus on your breathing when you are meditating.

This may seem like a lot of spiritual mumbo jumbo, but it isn't. Your breath indicates your state of mind. It's like the beat of a car engine. An experienced mechanic will be able to tell whether something is wrong with your car engine just by listening to it.

When you are out of breath, you cannot think straight. When you are angry or agitated, you find it hard to breathe or you breathe heavily or irregularly. You can tell the difference between an experienced athlete and an amateur runner by the way he or she breathes while running. There is a certain cadence, a natural rhythm, that you notice in the way they breathe even after running for a while. They are never out of breath.

When you are learning to sing or act or are attending a public speaking course, gaining an understanding of the correct way to breathe is important. They teach you how to breathe deep through your nose, silently and from your stomach.

Learning to breathe the right way will help you stay conscious of your breathing and also improve your concentration. Your brain uses about 20 per cent of the oxygen that you breathe. So, the more efficiently you breathe, the better the supply of oxygen to your brain, resulting in better concentration. Similarly, blood circulation is affected by the supply of oxygen. That's why, if you breathe correctly, in a rhythmic and natural manner, you will have more strength and stamina to perform physical tasks. When your muscles don't receive enough oxygen supply, they start to cramp, feel fatigued and become stiff. Therefore, when you are in pain, or feel frustrated or angry, it helps to breathe deeply, in and out. It regulates the supply of oxygen to your brain and muscles, thereby helping you relax and regain your equilibrium.

Focusing on your breath and calming your mind is a practical way to achieve clarity and focus.

There Is No Failure, Only Feedback

A child learning to walk often falls. Not once, but many times. It's inevitable. A child learning to walk without falling is unheard of. Yet, when a person tries to do something and fails, we label him or her a failure. This is wrong. The person is not a failure. It's only his or her actions that have failed. The way you use language and form a thought in your mind influence the way you perceive the consequences of your action. Have you heard of the phrase, 'Grace under pressure?' Do you know what it means? When nothing seems to be going right, when all the odds are stacked against you, when everyone has lost their faith in you, but you still keep your head on your shoulders and continue to try without losing your temper, your mind or your control, you are performing with courage. You are then performing with grace under pressure.

Would you call someone who has more than 1000 patents to his credit a failure? One of the greatest inventors, Thomas Edison, never admitted his failure. 'I have not failed,' he said. 'I have just found 10,000 ways that won't work.' He further said, 'Many of life's failures are people who did not realize how close they were to success when they gave up.' How we perceive different situations in our minds influences our future actions.

When you look at someone affluent, you think that he/she is blessed or that he/she has a gift which has made them successful. The truth is that for every triumph which you see, there are hundreds or thousands of failed attempts that you don't see. The list of businesses that I've attempted, started, even operated for a while and then closed could fill more than a few pages. I was a serial entrepreneur even before the term became fashionable. Some of the businesses that I started were way ahead of their time. They didn't sustain because the time was not right. I did not have the patience to watch the tide turn in my favour. I put them down as lessons learnt. I moved on. I didn't throw up my hands and give up. I tried something again and again to see if it worked. Once I was convinced that it didn't work, I moved on to something else. And right now, I'm a successful trainer. I hold my seminars across the world. When you take a very close look at success, you realize that it is nothing but an accumulation of what most people call failure but, as seen by the successful person, they are feedback for achieving success in the future.

The basketball legend, Michael Jordan, once said, 'I've missed more than 9000 shots in my career. I've lost almost 300 games. Twenty-six times I've been trusted to take the winning shot and I've missed. I've failed over and over and over again in my life. And that is why I succeed.' It takes courage to look at your failed attempts, acknowledge them, count them but not allow them to get the better of you. The key to success lies in how you emotionally respond to the results of your actions. If they don't produce the desired result, does it energize you to try again or does it deflate your energy?

When you experience failure, do you apply that label to yourself? When you fail, do you take it to heart or do you take it as a feedback for your actions, analyse it and figure out why your actions did not produce the desired results?

There are two types of emotions, positive and negative. Love, hope, faith, happiness, curiosity, enthusiasm, empathy, interest—these are all positive emotions. Anger, blame, fear, hatred, regret, resentment, shame, grief, worry—these are the negative ones. Recognize the negative emotions when you experience them, and try to overcome them. If you don't control them, they will give rise to more negative emotions and prevent you from achieving success.

When you feel angry at someone, instead of saying, 'I am angry', say 'I feel angry at _____. Why?' Try to analyse why you are feeling angry and the cause for it. Observe your emotional state and try to analyse it in a calm and collected manner. Once you learn how to observe your emotions, you will realize that you can stay passionate and yet be in control. Similarly, when you feel worried, don't say, 'I am worried.' Instead, ask yourself, 'What is causing this sense of worry?'

You will soon realize that very often, worry is just an irrational fear or sense of uncertainty masquerading as an emotion. You will recognize worry for what it really is—just a hollow voice distracting you from your purpose.

By identifying and observing your emotions in this way, you can immediately nip the negative ones in the bud and not let them grow into something you cannot control. **Learn how your identity controls everything you think, every emotion you experience and every action you take with the help of my guidance on www.wherewillyoubein5years.com.** Remember how hard your mind tried not to think about the red car? Instead of struggling with your negative emotions, observe them in an objective fashion. You can transform them into the energy you need for attempting again to achieve success.

Give Your Attention to What Matters

When you are reading a storybook or novel, especially if it is a whodunnit or when the plot has mystery and intrigue, you are tempted to skip ahead and look at the last pages to see the outcome. Isn't that so? But if you skip ahead, you spoil the whole experience of reading the story. If your experiences in life are not giving you what you want, change them. If you hate your job, find a new one; if your relationship is not working out, create new experiences.

The point I am trying to make is that you should change the experience if it no longer works for you. Life is too short to read stories that you don't enjoy, or watch movies that are not worth watching or go on holidays where, instead of relaxing, you get even more stressed. You can change the book, you can watch another movie, you can visit another place, you can make new friends, you can make new goals, but you are who you are, who you think you are. You can change the way you perceive yourself. You are a failure if you, and only you, say so. You are a success waiting to happen if you believe in it.

Muhammad Ali did not say, 'I am the greatest', after others told him he was. No, he said it even before he became a boxing champion. He said, 'I am the greatest' not after winning a match but before every match, because he believed he could win. *Self-belief is more important and more powerful than any other form of external validation or approval by other people.*

Your life is too short to dwell on what you failed to achieve or to do what will not lead to success. Let's go back to the list of things you wanted to do in life. Look at your list, go through the points and decide what is important and what needs your immediate attention. Ask yourself these questions:

1. How long will it take me to do this or achieve this goal? Will it take one year, three years or three years? Then categorize them accordingly.
2. What steps can I take *now* to achieve them? Then, list out the immediate steps that you can take to prepare for the eventual result.
3. Are there any goals in your list that you have attempted to achieve in the past but did not succeed? Analyse them and ask yourself if they are worth attempting again or whether you should let them go.

You start reading a story from the first page, the beginning. You don't start a book from the middle or start watching a movie from any random scene, do you? Then, why attempt to do something without making the necessary preparations? Goals are achievable when they are clear in your mind.

In the next chapter, we will take a closer look at goals, and examine the art of setting goals that are achievable.

5

Setting Your Goals

'The fight is won or lost far away from the witnesses—behind the lines, in the gym, and out there on the road, long before I dance under those lights.'

— Muhammad Ali

Have you ever got lost in a new neighbourhood or in a new city? You are going in a certain direction and you come to a crossroads or a fork in the road, you pick one and then later take a turn or two, and suddenly you get a feeling of déjà vu. You realize that the surroundings look familiar. You are back in the same place from where you had initially started. You obviously took a wrong turn, ended up going around in a circle and then returned to your starting point.

Did You Lose Your Way?

First of all, though you knew where you wanted to go, you didn't really 'know' the way to get there. That is, in theory, you knew the route on a map or you knew the directions roughly but you were not exactly familiar with the way because you had never physically travelled on it before. The second factor to consider here is that you probably took a wrong turn or missed a turn. In other words, you were distracted or your attention wandered and you failed to follow or apply the directions. There's also a third possible reason. You were misguided. The map you were using was probably wrong because it was old and had not been updated with some of the new roads.

It's okay to lose your way when you are on holiday in a new city. It could be enjoyable because you would see streets and places off the beaten track. However, if you are going for a job interview or to attend a meeting or even a social function, then, you will probably get late, miss an opportunity or an occasion and also end up wasting time and energy.

Failing to Plan Is Planning to Fail

Have you heard of the term 'recce'? It means to carry out reconnaissance or conduct a survey. The term is said to have originated from the military, where special troops would be sent to survey or assess a place or a situation ahead of an actual attack or operation.

In engineering and logistics, it is standard practice to conduct a recce before building a road or a bridge, or transporting goods across a new route. Even in show business, before actually shooting on location, the production team does a recce to ensure it is suitable and fits the script or the director's vision.

The advantage of conducting a recce is that you can explore options or ways in which you can get to a place, make or do something before you actually go on a journey or a mission or perform an action. In other words, it is like a trial run or a dress rehearsal before hosting an actual event or function. It enables you to predict all potential obstacles or shortcomings, prepares you to overcome them and also ensures that everything goes smoothly and according to the plan. You are also able to gather information in advance on how much time and resources will be required for the event or the operation, thus enabling you to allocate enough for both.

You can also abandon the mission or operation in case you realize during the recce that it is not going to work out or that the risks involved are not worth taking. This prevents you from investing too much time, effort and resources; it even reduces the risks of losing hope or becoming disheartened or disappointed.

In essence, you are paving the way for success by preparing in advance and doing something the right way. It is somewhat like taking a car for a test drive before buying it, or going out for a few dates with someone before you propose to or commit to spending your entire life with them.

Set Your Goals to Get There

You need to set your goals in such a manner that you have a good shot at achieving success, at the same time making sure that you don't lose your way or waste your time and energy. In the previous chapter, we looked at the importance of making a list and writing down what you want to do or achieve.

Many people have told me that, despite writing down their goals diligently, they still don't get close to achieving their goals. Why is that? When someone tells me they are having trouble accomplishing their goals even after having written them down, I usually ask them some questions and follow it up with some advice. The conversation usually goes something like this:

Are you doing something or taking action about your goal or what you can do to achieve a particular goal? Let's say you want to lose weight? That is your goal. Writing it down is not enough. You need to define why you want to lose weight and how you are going to do it.

The 'why' is to motivate you and also to establish or verify whether losing weight is something that you really need right now. Imagine someone who isn't fat or is already in ideal shape attempting to lose weight. The result could be anorexia or some other health complications.

Do you know how many kilos or pounds you want to lose? Are you willing to commit to a diet and an exercise regimen? Do you have a time frame for achieving your goal? Sometimes our ambitions or our ideals get the better of us, and we end up setting targets that are practically not possible to accomplish within the said time frame.

I knew someone who felt miserable because he could not afford to bring his aged parents to live with him in the city where he worked. They were living in a village which was quite far away, and he could afford to visit them only once or twice a year.

He said his goal was to make enough money so that he could afford a bigger apartment in the city for his parents. I asked him if, at his current salary and earnings, he could save or spare enough funds to do that. His answer was no. I asked him if in a year he could save enough to rent a bigger apartment. Again the answer was no. I asked if he could do it in three years. He shook his head. I asked him if he could do it in five years. He said, 'Maybe.' Then he broke down in tears. He said that they might not live that long.

My advice to him was that there was no point feeling miserable about a situation which he didn't have the power to change. He could set a five-year goal to save enough funds to bring his aged parents to stay with him. Or he could quit his job in the city and find employment closer to where his parents lived. He might not earn as much but at least he would have the satisfaction of being there to take care of them.

These were his options. Feeling miserable about it was not going to help.

If there is nothing you can do about your goal right now or in the immediate future, then, stop fretting about it or at least set it aside for the time being.

Goal Setting, Simplified

When we talk about setting goals, it is generally understood that one simply has to write down one's goals. This may seem pretty straightforward and easy but it isn't because writing down your goals is not enough.

There are many people who make New Year's resolutions year after year, but they never achieve them. Why? They are obviously doing something wrong. Either they lack motivation to follow through or they are unrealistic and set goals that they are not really committed to achieving.

Let us examine the right way to do it and to identify potential pitfalls that you need to avoid while setting your goals. Later on, we will explore some interesting ways to bring your goals to life and will focus on how to transform them into an inspiring, consistent and motivating presence in your everyday life.

So, here are three golden guidelines for setting goals.

1. Are Your Goals SMART?

Most people already know what the acronym SMART stands for, but surprisingly this is still one of the most ignored rules or guidelines when it comes to setting goals.

SMART stands for specific, measurable, actionable, realistic and time-bound. After you have written down a goal, use this yardstick to evaluate it and see if it fulfils your criteria. If your goals are SMART, then, you have a better chance of achieving them.

Specific: Ask yourself whether you have defined your goal in a specific and clear manner. For example, if your goal is to make more money, you need to specify how much is 'more'. Do you have a figure in mind? Is it a hundred thousand or 1 million? How do you intend to do it? Do you intend to earn more or spend less and save more?

Measurable: Ensure that your goal is something you can quantify or define in terms that can be measured or compared. Let's say, you set a goal to eat healthier. How do you measure healthier food? Do you count the calories? Do you see whether your meals have all the essential elements like proteins, vitamins, carbohydrates, and so on? Do you ensure that you have meals that contain fresh fruits and vegetables, and regulate the number of times you eat meat?

Actionable: Do you have a plan of action to achieve your goal? If your goal is to quit smoking, then, how are you going to do it? Are you going to use a nicotine patch? Are you going to try counselling? Do you have a step-by-step approach whereby you will reduce the number of cigarettes you smoke in a day? What about temptations? What steps are you going to take to resist or overcome the need to smoke? How are you going to keep yourself motivated and committed when you are faced with these temptations?

Realistic: This is a very delicate aspect. While it is good to be ambitious, you need to do a reality check to make sure you are not day-dreaming or fantasizing. For instance, it would be unrealistic for someone who has just started carpentry and woodwork to build a boat. It would make sense first to make something smaller, like a chair or a table, to test and prove your abilities before attempting a boat. Another example could be that of someone who is learning how to drive; it makes sense to learn to do so on an empty road or lane rather than in the midst of heavy traffic.

Time-bound: This is very important. Here's a simple way to classify your goals.

After you write down your goals, put them into three categories:

a. The ones you can accomplish in a year's time.
b. Those which will take between one and three years.
c. Those for which you need at least five years.

If there are any goals for which you need more than five years, then, it would make sense to put them aside and attend to the ones that are more immediately attainable. **You will come across many such amazing exercises in my 'Where Will You Be in Five Years' online course, available on www.wherewillyoubein5years.com.** Writing down a goal without setting a specific time frame is like making a wish and not trying. If your goal is to become a millionaire, then, figure out how long it will take you to achieve it. If your goal is to build a business, then, define how many years it will take you to set it up. Go through each stage of growth, such as planning, development, production, marketing, etc.

2. Do You Have Too Many Goals?

Giving importance to quantity over quality is a common mistake when setting goals. Do you know why advertising billboards don't have more than three to five words on them? A message which is more than six to eight words long is easy to forget as compared to a message which is three to five words long.

Do you know why they used to break a play or drama into as many as five acts? So that every time the curtain went down, the audience would get an opportunity to process the story they had watched on stage. This is the same reason why movies and concerts have an interval midway. It is not easy to sustain the attention of an audience for too long without a break. Similarly, sports, games or matches are interrupted so that players can refresh their energies and rethink their strategies.

If you attempt too many goals in a short period of time, you will most likely end up disappointed. Even if you did accomplish a few of them, your success would be tinged with disappointment for the ones you could not attempt or did not achieve.

Have you heard of the Pareto principle? Also known as the 80/20 rule, it is so named after Vilfredo Pareto, an Italian economist who observed that 80 per cent of the land in Italy was owned by 20 per cent of the people. Many parallels to this rule were then observed by researchers in different fields as diverse as nature, finance and marketing. So for instance, it was found that 80 per cent of the peas produced in a garden were from 20 per cent of the pods harvested. About 80 per cent of the profits of a company came from 20 per cent of the customers. Similarly, about 80 per cent of the sales of an organization were achieved by 20 per cent of the sales team.

It is to be noted that the 80/20 rule is an observation and not an absolute. It could be 70/30 or 75/25. It means that you can achieve more by focusing on a few things that are important rather than attempting a whole lot of things, dissipating your energy and diluting the effort.

It is therefore important to make a long list of goals, re-evaluate them in order of importance and then make a short list. Ideally, you should not have more than three to five goals at one point in time so that you are able to focus better.

3. Do You Review Your Goals on a Regular Basis?

This is very important. What happens if you take your eyes off the road while driving? That's right. Your attention is diverted, and you could lose control and cause an accident. Similarly, if you forget about your goal after setting it, you might as well bid goodbye to it.

The effort and time you invest in planning and preparing for your goal goes to waste if you let your attention wander and lose your focus. You need to be constantly aware of your goal to remain motivated to pursue and accomplish it. How do you ensure this? By creating a reminder that tells you why you want this goal.

This is where a vision board comes in. A vision board is a very effective tool to create awareness about your goal. This will inspire you to take action and in turn produce results.

What Is a Vision Board?

It is not enough to put your goals on paper, you need to bring your goals to life by illuminating them with a visual and tangible appeal.

A vision board is a visual representation of your goal. Let us say, your goal is to become a successful musician. So, you consider all the visual cues that will motivate you to practise and perform to your full potential. For example, you can collect the pictures of your role models and create a collage of them. Then you can add inspirational quotes by those people. Your dream might be to perform at some famous venues or theatres. Take pictures of those venues and add them to the collage.

All these are different elements of your vision board. You could add the awards and accolades that are given to outstanding musicians as something to aspire to. If you are aware of some special rituals followed by other musicians in their daily practice, you could visually represent them on your vision board.

For example, I once knew a pianist whose teacher believed that, while playing the piano, if your fingers moved in a smooth motion, without any sudden movement to break the rhythm, it reflected in the quality of your musical output. So she made her students practise by balancing a coin on the back of their hands, just above their fingers.

The pianist, whose goal was to achieve excellence in her field, created a vision board which included a close-up photograph of a pair of hands poised over a keyboard with a coin balanced on top. This was a constant reminder to her of the discipline that she was required to cultivate in order to achieve her goal to reach the top of her field.

Use your creativity and ingenuity to create replicas of your vision board so that you are constantly reminded of your goals. For instance, you could take a digital image of your vision board and use it as your display picture on your social networking site or as a screen saver on your smartphone.

Having a vision makes you dream big. Imagine a wonderful life ahead and take steps towards your vision. This is where your journey begins. Simple steps can lead to extraordinary journeys.

6

Eight Steps to a Better You

'Success is liking yourself, liking what you do, and liking how you do it.'

— Maya Angelou

A thousand-mile journey begins with one step, followed by another. Similarly, you have to build your life bit by bit, one day after another. Sure, you can take a leap once in a while. But most of the time, you take one step at a time. That's how you design your life. You consider every aspect of your life and then, make small changes every day. Over a period of time, in a year, in three years or in five years, you will achieve what is called a transformation which will change your life for the better.

When you consider the different aspects in the wheel of life, you realize that there is always the temptation to focus on what's more visible than what's more practical. Let us examine each of the eight different aspects in the wheel of life and see how your choices influence them.

Each aspect of your life—health, financial situation, career, dating life or romantic relationships, learning curve or journey of personal growth, possessions and the environment they create, fun and leisure and friends and family—needs to be nurtured and treated in such a manner that your life moves at a well-balanced and meaningful pace.

So, let's take a look at these eight aspects, and try to understand how paying attention to them can improve your life.

1. Take Control of Your Health

Your health is primarily defined by the food you eat and your lifestyle. You are more likely to become fat if you eat more junk food. So, to reduce that weight you go on a crash diet. After that, you feel that you deserve to indulge and end up binge-eating to make up for the drastic diet measures and put on more pounds than you had lost.

Similarly, you go to the gym and exercise regularly for a month. You see visible results in how you look and how you feel. Then life takes over. You become busy; for the next eleven months you work late, watch too much TV, get up late, and have no time to go to the gym. What happened? You made an ambitious attempt and then lost sight of your goal. You made a huge effort but failed to keep it up.

Now let's say you cut down one unhealthy item from your diet every week. The first week, you give up donuts, the next week pizzas, the week after chocolates, and so on. In the next six months, you eliminate all processed foods that contain sugar and replace them with fruits and vegetables. You maintain this consistently and eventually you will see that it has produced literally life-changing results.

In the same manner, you can make an effort to discipline your exercise activities. In the first month, go to the gym three days a week for one hour. The next month, make it four days a week. Then, five days a week and finally six days a week.

Do you realize that when you make small changes, they tend to remain consistent, and you are more likely to stay committed? That is how you build a house, a fortune or a life.

2. Grow Your Wealth in a Steady Manner

Your finances are influenced by how you spend or save every month. You can have a grand goal of making a million dollars, but if you wait for a big opportunity to make that money all at once, you might end up waiting forever. Instead, if you focus on your spending habits and make it a point to save a small percentage of your earnings, over a period of time, you will be much closer to your goal. In the first year, you may be able to save just a few thousands, but in the next year, you will make better progress if you increase the percentage of your savings.

If you invest wisely, you will earn compound interest which will enable you to multiply the value of your savings. Depending on the risk you are willing to take, you can invest by choosing to protect your capital or go for a higher rate of return.

As any financial analyst will tell you, in the short term, you are likely to risk some losses if the market turns against your investments. However, if you spread your investments across instruments, in the long run, your losses will even out and you will make a profit. Keeping track of your expenses also helps. The basic rules are very simple: don't spend more than you earn; don't put all your eggs in one basket; don't try to make a quick buck with questionable schemes but stay invested in schemes with a long-standing performance record.

All this seems so absurdly easy, isn't it? Yet why do people end up in dire straits? That is because they are all in a hurry to make those million dollars.

When you make a fortune the right way, you are investing in a habit, in a lifestyle choice. You are being consistent, prudent and practical. You are choosing quality over quantity. You are not just trying to get rich, but you are growing your wealth.

3. How Passionate Are You about Your Work?

When we meet someone for the first time, the second or third question usually is: 'What do you do for a living?' Why do we ask this? Do you really care about what the other person does for a living? If someone tells you that he/she is a rocket scientist, you are more likely to be impressed than if he/she is in a profession like teaching. Isn't that so? The point is that we judge people by their profession but not by how passionate or committed they are to what they do.

'It must be so exciting to be a rocket scientist,' you say by way of making conversation. The other person replies, 'Oh, not really, it's just a job like any other job.' Why do we assume that a scientist has a better job than, say, a teacher? It's because we don't get to meet a rocket scientist every day, whereas if you are a parent, you have probably already met more than a fair number of teachers. Something that is rare is exotic, and therefore we expect it to be exciting and even highly rewarding.

Apart from that, it is also the higher status that some jobs have than others and the amount of money a person makes. We know that a rocket scientist makes more than a teacher, so we assume that it is better to be a scientist than a teacher. That is a very wrong assumption, and it is exactly the reason why most people are unhappy in their careers. Even though they are quite good at what they do, they are not happy because they do not understand the purpose of their jobs. They think it is just a job.

Some wise man once said that if you choose a job that you love, you won't have to work for the rest of your life. I would rather put it this way: If someone puts a gun to your head and says you have to spend six to eight hours working, what work would you choose? Choose your career wisely, not because you want to make money doing it but because you will be spending an awful amount of your life doing it.

It's not about how much money you make, it's about how you do your job, how much your job matters to you, how much of a difference you can make in the lives of others. That is when your job becomes meaningful.

You can make more money than anybody else you know and still be unhappy if you don't believe that what you do is important or meaningful. You can make less money than most people but still be proud of what you do and command respect if what you do makes a difference in the lives of others. Your choice of career doesn't define your life. The passion that you feel every time you go to work is what defines your life.

Try this simple test to find out how passionate you are about what you do. Every morning, ask yourself: Is this what I want to do today? If your answer is yes, then you have obviously made the right career choice. **If no, then find three reasons that make you feel the way you do. Check out www.wherewillyoubein5years.com to get clarity on your passion.**

4. When Someone Knows You Better than You Know Yourself

If you are married or in a relationship, you are either happy you found the right person or you constantly wonder whether you are with the right person or not. If you are still dating, then, you probably compare and judge the people with whom you go out.

No one is perfect. No one is right all the time. Each one of us has our own set of idiosyncrasies or quirks. Why then are we so obsessed with being with or finding Ms/Mr Right? We know that despite all our faults and failings, there will be someone who will love us for who we are. So, when we meet such a person, we think of him or her as the right person for us. For others, that person might be completely and utterly wrong, but for you that person is right. This is why romance is the subject of most stories. It never fails to fascinate us. It's something we have been trying to figure out for ages.

Why one person is attracted to another is one of the biggest mysteries and also one of the biggest miracles in this world. If you ask people what romance means to them, you will get a variety of answers. Even two people who are in a relationship might disagree on what romance means to each of them.

For a couple who has been together for five years, flowers, candlelit dinners or chocolates may signify romance. For two people who have been with each other for fifty years, it could be something else altogether, perhaps the way a person smiles or laughs or the way they look at you.

When it comes to designing the romantic aspect of your life, you need to keep in mind two things. The first one is self-awareness. You should know that you are important but you are also imperfect. So, whether you are looking for a romantic partner or you are already in a relationship, examine how much your ego and level of self-awareness are influencing your life. If you are aware of only your good qualities but are ignoring your imperfections, then, you have no right to blame others if your relationship is failing. You don't have to be perfect. You just have to be aware of the fact that you are not and accept it. Once you know your shortcomings, you will be able to see yourself from the other person's point of view.

The second thing to focus on is your expectations. You have an image in your mind of what your partner should be like. Most often, we assume that the other person will live up to our expectations. This is when most relationships fail. It is important to share and modify expectations. Sometimes our expectations can help our partner improve his/her life and personality. Sometimes our expectations can put a strain on both our life and relationships.

For instance, expecting flowers from your partner on a special occasion might seem like a normal thing. However if, after a while, either of you thinks that it is becoming a stale tradition, you should be willing to try something new. You should be prepared to change and give the other person something new to look forward to.

Similarly, expecting something in return for a gesture is another common form of expectation. When you do something nice, such as give your partner flowers, you expect a favour in return. Give and take might be the norm in other types of relationships. However, this is not how romantic relationships work. If you are nice to your partner because you enjoy it, then, you are truly in love. If you are nice to them because you expect something in return, then, it's a form of manipulation. Romantic relationships can suffer if you are manipulative. Sooner or later, your partner will see through it. True love is easy when you love someone. It's hard to fake it. Communication is the key to a successful relationship. Talk frankly and as often as you can. You will be surprised by the things you learn about yourself and also about your partner.

5. Stay Curious and You Will Enjoy Life

If you look at the lives of great people, you will realize that most of them were lifelong learners. Learning and personal growth are essential to succeed in life. They go hand in hand. Most of us are lucky because we spend the first two to three decades of our life learning. Our learning does not and should not stop once we leave school or college and step into a job or what is called the real world. Our education should continue all through our lives. They say you cannot teach an old dog new tricks. It is a myth probably spread by lazy people that you cannot learn new things when you are old. In fact, the more you learn, the sharper your mind and body become.

Mastering extra skills will not only help you perform better in your job, but also help you earn more doing what you do. In many professional fields, continuous learning is the only way to maintain your employability. Learning does not necessarily always mean acquiring a skill which will help you in your career. It can also help you lead a better life.

For instance, research shows that people who know how to play a musical instrument are less likely to suffer from brain-related disorders, such as Alzheimer's or dementia when they grow old. Similarly, people who play board games like chess or Scrabble have stronger mental acuity when they grow old.

This implies that when you love learning and you continue to learn, you start appreciating the finer things of life. Learning how to play an instrument or enjoying a social game that involves pitting your intelligence against another person's makes your mind agile, and you realize that it is an enjoyable experience.

Don't lose opportunities to learn. In this day and age, you can learn almost anytime and anywhere. Download an audio book on your portable music player or smartphone and listen to it while you are waiting for your dental appointment. Make friends with people who you think are smarter than you and know more than you do. Read something that you enjoy and learn from it.

6. Things Belong to You, You Don't Belong to Them

You feel good when you buy a new smartphone. The feeling, however, lasts only for a few moments or at the most for a few days. Let's say you have bought the phone using your credit card. For how long will you have to pay for it?

When we desire to buy or possess something, we should ask ourselves: How is this possession going to improve the quality of my life? Is it worth the money I am paying for it? This is not to say that you should shun all material possessions. No, acquiring what is important and necessary can improve your life and also enhance your sense of achievement, fulfilment and success. If your old car is not giving you good mileage, then, it makes sense to buy a new one which will. If buying a new dress will help you impress your colleagues and your clients and help you progress in your career, then, it is something you should invest in. If buying a house in a specific locality will enable your children to go to a better school, then, it is a worthwhile investment.

You should exercise prudence when you buy things, not shun all material possessions.

I once visited the office of a manager of a shopping mall. There was a poster on the wall, which read, 'You haven't sold anything, if you haven't sold someone something that he didn't need.' Advertising, the media, salespersons and supermarkets are always trying to sell you things that you don't really need. What you want and what you need are two entirely different things. Learn how to differentiate between the two, and you will start investing in things that matter. Surround yourself with possessions that enhance your life. *Do not surround yourself with things that distract you from living your life.*

7. How to Be Creative? Play Games

There was a time when the workplace was a sacred zone. It was all about business. The office was a place where you went to work, not to enjoy yourself, socialize or be creative. The knowledge economy changed that. Companies, such as Amazon and Google, created spaces within the workplace where employees could relax, let off steam, play games and enjoy. Why did they do this? It's because those companies recognized the importance of playing and having fun.

Fun, leisure and recreational activities are as important in life as doing meaningful and purposeful work. The T-shirt message, 'Work Hard, Play Harder', summarizes the importance of maintaining a balance between work and play.

When we were children, we never lost an opportunity to enjoy ourselves. And we never felt guilty about it. As we grew older, we were conditioned to avoid leisure unless we had earned it. If we spent a weekday playing golf or doing nothing, we would hide it from others because we felt we were doing something wrong.

Companies have now realized that combining play with work can help relieve stress, improve productivity, boost creativity, stimulate team work and social interaction between employees, and empower people. Even in my seminars, I ask my audience to participate in a variety of games and activities. As the old saying goes, 'We don't stop playing games because we grow old. We grow old because we stop playing games.'

It is important to take a vacation and spend time with your family and friends once in a while. After all, you are not living on an island. You are living in a community, and the people around you matter. This brings us to the last but definitely not the least aspect of our life.

8. Stay Tuned to Your Social Support System

Whom do you talk to when you want to confide or seek advice? Your family and friends, right? When you hear some good news, what do you want to do? You want to share it with your near and dear ones. On a festive occasion, a birthday or an anniversary, you invite your friends and family to have a good time. When you are afraid of something, worried about something, or need advice, you go to a family member or a trusted friend.

We create a social support system by cultivating new friends and staying in touch with our family members. Of course, you don't get to choose your family but you do get to choose your friends. It is important to acknowledge the position your family holds in your life. After all, they brought you up and gave you the values that you endorse. Your beliefs and personality are shaped by how you interact with your family.

As time passes, and sometimes because of misunderstandings, people drift apart. However, it is important to stay in touch with your family. Your life is enriched by the relationships you build and maintain through the years. From our friends, we learn the comfort of companionship. Your friends and family know you as the person you really are and accept you as you are, with all your imperfections. You feel at home in their company.

Research indicates that people who have a strong social support system are not likely to be depressed or unhappy. If you have strong and close ties with friends and family, being with them can enhance your happiness and improve your zest for life.

It isn't enough to stay in touch with your family and friends on a social network site. Meeting them in person and having a face-to-face conversation can never be replaced with messaging or clicking a 'like' button. Make a list of people you know and against each name write down their birthdays and anniversaries. If you don't know their birthday or anniversary, find out. It is pretty easy to do this if you are connected to them on a social network site.

Do you call your friends or family members only when you need them? Do you call them only when you need their advice or help, never just to talk or catch up? This is not how you create a social support system. Make it a habit to call your friends and family members and wish them on special occasions. Make it a habit to meet at least one family member, relative or friend every week. You don't need an occasion.

You can just call them up and meet them for a cup of coffee or invite them home for dinner.

* * *

Talking of habits, do you realize that when we think of habits, we mostly think about bad habits? Why is that? Is it because most of us have more bad habits than good ones? In our next chapter, we will examine how our habits influence our life, and how, by cultivating certain power habits, we can create a better future.

7

Ten Must-have Power Habits

'We are what we repeatedly do. Excellence then is not an act but a habit.'

— Aristotle

Change your habits if you want to change your life. The bad news is that changing an existing habit or giving it up is not easy. The good news is that beginning a new habit or cultivating it is not that hard. Let's consider a typical workday or weekday in your life (this is just a hypothetical sketch of an average day in the life of an average person. Your typical workday or weekday could be, and hopefully is, very different from what is described here).

The alarm goes off at 6 a.m. and you push the snooze button. You do this every day because you know that it is okay if you get up half an hour later, at 6.30. You can still get to work on time if you rush through your morning routine. You force yourself to get up at 6.30 and go to the bathroom. You look at the clock or your watch at least two to three times, once while getting dressed and then again while having breakfast. Just when you are about to get out of your house, you realize that you can't find your car key. You look for it on the coffee table, the dining table, the bedside table and even under the bed. You look for it on the sofa, check whether it's wedged between the cushions. No luck. You look at the clock again. You are late. You bump your knee against a chair and swear out loudly. Your day is having a bad start.

When Things Start to Go Wrong, They Keep On Going Wrong

You scratch your head, and try to remember what you did the previous night; where you could have put the car key. Suddenly, it dawns on you. You think you know where it could be. You rush to the laundry bin and pick up the trousers you had been wearing yesterday, and which you had put there to be washed later. Hey presto, you've found it. The key is in one of the pockets. While fishing out the key, you also find a few crumpled-up currency notes and a piece of chewing gum still in its wrapper. You stuff the money in your wallet, pop the chewing gum into your mouth and rush out the door. Once again, while getting into the car, you look at your watch. You are running a bit late but with some luck on the road, you might just make it in time for work.

However, the situation is completely different on the road. It looks like the other people are in no great hurry to get anywhere. The vehicles ahead of you are moving at a snail's pace. You can hear the car behind you honking. You glance at the rear-view mirror, and see that the guy behind the wheel is clenching his fists. You turn up the radio volume as the traffic news comes on. Oh! The report says that a car has broken down up ahead and that's why the traffic is being held up.

You glance at your watch again, and now you are sure that you are not going to make it in time for a meeting you had scheduled for 10.30 a.m. You decide to call the office and let them know that you are running late. While talking on your cell phone, you see that the car behind is giving an indicator to change lanes and get into the left lane. It suddenly occurs to you that there is an interchange up ahead where you can take a left to get to your office.

The driver of the car behind is probably thinking along the same lines. You see a gap opening, and turn the steering wheel to change lanes. Suddenly, there is a loud sound. The vehicle just behind has banged right into your car. You curse and drop the phone. There is a medley of honks as you step out of your car. Tempers fly and a road rage incident not worth describing ensues. After what seems like a few minutes of yelling in order to reason with the other guy, both of you end up exchanging phone numbers so that you can sort this out later with your respective insurance companies.

When you get back to the car, you realize that you still haven't called your office even though it is almost 10 a.m. You look for your cell phone which you had dropped when the accident took place. You can't find it on the seat and realize that it must have rolled on to the floor. You can't risk looking for it now. So you start your car and carefully move ahead. Not even half the day is over, and you are already stressed and tired. You wish you had made an early start and avoided the rush hour. You wish you had not wasted time looking for your car key. You wish you had woken up early.

How to Begin Your Day

This is not how anyone should begin their day. Try and identify at least three bad habits that caused the delay, the stress and the accident. What were they? The first one was, of course, hitting the snooze button. It's a bad habit because it creates unpredictability and disruption in your schedule. It is also pointless because you are hardly getting any real rest or sleep by hitting the snooze button for ten minutes more or thirty minutes more. Your sleep is already disturbed. You might as well have set the alarm for 6.30 a.m. if you really wanted to sleep that much longer. Do you see what happened here? You made a plan but you failed to stick to it. You changed the plan without any reason, just because you felt you could get away with changing it. It's okay to change plans if you are going to get better results than originally intended. However, changing a plan to find out whether you can achieve the same result is not only foolish but a waste of time.

The second bad habit that you need to change is keeping your things anywhere, in a random manner. If you have a key hook on the wall right next to the entrance door and you hang your key on the hook every time you come back home, you will never lose it or waste your time looking for it. Putting things in a proper place is a good habit to cultivate. How many times have you been frustrated because you couldn't find the TV remote or your phone charger? Why couldn't you find these items? Either you don't have a proper place for them and that's why they are left lying around, or you have a place for them but you haven't developed the habit of putting them in their respective places.

Emptying your pockets before taking off your clothes is another good habit to have. Going through the pockets of your clothes before you put them in the laundry bin or washing machine is another. This way you won't have to iron out any wet and crumpled currency notes or deal with stains from pens or candy left behind in your pocket.

Talking on the phone while driving is the third bad habit you need to change. If you hadn't been talking on the phone while driving, you wouldn't have lost your focus and the accident could have been averted. Accidents happen when we lose focus. We lose focus when we allow other things or situations to distract us from our task. Multitasking was all the rage a few years ago. People boasted about how they could do two or more things at a time. Research proves otherwise. You can do as many things as you want at the same time, but if you really want results then, you have to focus on one thing at a time. Multitasking makes you look busy but, at the end of the day, you don't have anything to show. No results.

Do you think Michelangelo was thinking about what he would have for lunch when he was painting the Sistine Chapel ceiling? No, he was concentrating on each brushstroke and nothing else. Do you think a chess player will answer his e-mails or update his social networking profile while his or her opponent makes the next move? No, you make a move and immediately think of all the possible moves that your opponent will make so that you can decide your next strategy.

Imagine another scenario where you don't hit the snooze button. You get up early, have a pleasant start to the day, beat the rush hour and reach office on time. You have a productive day with hardly any reason to feel stressed or worried. Every time you look at the clock, you don't feel hard-pressed but happy, confident and relaxed. There is plenty of time to do the things that you have planned.

Make Everything Work with Clockwork Precision

You don't have to think about where the car key is because it is where it usually is, hanging on the designated key hook next to the main door. There are no accidents, because you don't talk on the cell phone while driving.

Now, some people might consider such a well-planned and disciplined life dull and boring. To those who feel that way, you just have to point out the long-term consequences of having one bad day after another. It makes one feel frustrated and creates mental and physical anguish which could eventually lead to a mental breakdown or illness.

The Only Surprises Worth Having Are the Pleasant Ones

When you cultivate good habits and eliminate bad ones, you are more likely to find yourself in pleasant situations than unpleasant ones. If you put spurious fuel in your car, it will damage the engine. If you breathe smoke and polluted air, it will hurt your lungs and affect your health. If you continue with your bad habits, you will continue to fail in life. On the other hand, if you look after your car and service it regularly, it will never break down. If you keep your environment clean, you will have fresh air to breathe and feel energized. If you cultivate good habits, they will give you the power to achieve success.

How does one cultivate power habits to achieve success, and how does one eliminate bad ones? You just need to understand how habits are formed. Once you do this, you can take the necessary steps to get rid of habits that take you away from your goals, and adopt new ones that bring you closer to them.

Habits are the tasks that you perform without thinking or planning. Brushing your teeth in the morning or having a cup of coffee while reading a newspaper are a few examples. You don't have to plan the night before to brush your teeth in the morning, do you? Nor do you ever forget to brush your teeth. Why is that? Because it's a part of your daily routine. Similarly, you feel lost if you read your newspaper without your coffee, and the other way around.

Now, let's say you make a New Year's resolution to get up early in the morning and go for a walk or jog. You manage to do it for a few days, but after a while you again start sleeping late and skipping your walk or jog. What happened? You did not do it long enough to turn it into a habit.

You have been brushing your teeth every morning for as long as you remember. It is a habit which you cannot break, and it hardly requires any mental effort or reminder.

Try this. Don't brush your teeth tomorrow morning and see how you feel. You will feel embarrassed when you open your mouth to speak to other people. You might not immediately develop bad breath, but you will be aware of your breath and notice the difference the entire day.

Brushing your teeth regularly is a good habit. Now try the same experiment with a bad habit, such as smoking. Don't smoke for a day. Yes, it's not easy to do but try it and see how you feel. When you give up a good habit, you feel bad. When you give up a bad habit, you feel good. That's the difference. **Learn how to quit bad habits that can be harmful to you with the help of my video on www.wherewillyoubein5years.com.**

Understand How Habits Are Formed

Until an action is performed repeatedly—day in, day out—and until it becomes a habit, you need to set a reminder that motivates you to do it. So, to get up early in the morning and go for a walk, you first need to set an alarm the previous night; this means you have to plan for it in advance. To ensure that you get up early in the morning, you have to get enough sleep, which means you have to go to bed earlier.

Why did you make brushing your teeth a daily habit? You wanted to keep your teeth and gums healthy. That is the reward for brushing your teeth regularly. You need to use a reward to motivate yourself to perform an action repeatedly till it turns into a habit. The rewards for getting up early and going for a morning walk are many. You get an opportunity to spend time with yourself, to clear your mind, to gather your thoughts, see the sunrise and begin your day in a pleasant way. You need to use these rewards as constant reminders to perform the act of getting up early on a regular basis until it becomes a daily routine.

The three Rs of forming a habit are: reward, reminder and routine. Let's try to use these to inculcate a new habit, such as getting up early. Later, we'll also see how we can use these to get rid of an old bad habit. Make a list of all the benefits of getting up early: you will have a pleasant day; you won't have to hurry through your morning routine; you will get to watch the sunrise; you will be able to beat the morning peak hour, and so on. If all these benefits are not good enough, then, think about a specific reward to motivate yourself further. Let's say, if you get up at 6 a.m. every day in a row for ten consecutive days, then, on the eleventh day you give yourself a treat. The treat could be something as simple as a chocolate brownie or something grand such as a spa treatment or a new garment.

So, now you have a specific reward to motivate yourself to develop a new habit. However, it's not enough. You also need a reminder. You can have more than one reminder. For instance, you can set an alarm to remind yourself to go to sleep early on the previous night, so that you can get enough sleep and wake up refreshed the next morning. Similarly, you can set another reminder to wake you up the next morning.

On a calendar, mark the days you get up early or write them down in a journal. At the end of every week or every month review your progress. At some point, you will realize that the habit has become a part of your routine. Some habits take longer to settle in than others. It all depends on how enticing the rewards are, and how effective the reminders are.

How to Use the Three Rs to Quit a Habit

The reward–reminder–routine method can also be used to quit a habit. Let's take smoking. What are the rewards of smoking? There were obviously some 'rewards' of smoking, which is the reason you took it up in the first place and then continued to do it. It probably makes you feel cool in a circle of friends, calms your nerves, gives you something to do with your hands when you are sitting idle and thinking, and so on.

Now let's look at the disadvantages of smoking. It affects your mouth, throat, nose and lungs. If carried on for long, it can cause cancer. You are also wasting a lot of money on cigarettes.

Make a list of the advantages and the disadvantages and write them in two adjoining columns. Pin it up on the wall above your desk. This list of rewards and consequences is a reminder to give up smoking. However, you will realize that you need more than one reminder. The next time you feel the urge to smoke, use an alternative to cigarettes. It could be a strip of chewing gum, a walk around the block or even a glass of plain water. You also need to make a conscious effort to avoid the triggers that lead you to smoke or create a situation where you unconsciously take out a cigarette. The first step is to identify these triggers.

Ask yourself when do you feel the need to smoke and what makes you do it. Perhaps, you have a smoke with your morning cup of coffee. So, the coffee is a potential trigger. Try to substitute the cigarette with something else or have the coffee without the cigarette. You probably feel tempted in the company of others who smoke. So, avoid situations which put you in the company of smokers. You might have realized that you tend to smoke when you are stressed. Holding a cigarette in your hand calms you down. If so, then hold it but don't light it. Or you could squeeze a stress ball when you feel the urge to smoke.

Now comes the part where you break the routine or ritual. You may not be able to do it in the first attempt, but it will eventually happen if you keep at it. Make notes in a journal once you take the decision to quit a habit. Write down how many days you went without smoking in the first week. Perhaps, you succumbed to temptation once or twice; write this down. Go back and review your journal entries every week. You will see a pattern emerging. This progress will encourage you to persist in your efforts.

Remember, it all depends on the attractiveness of the rewards, the effectiveness of the reminders and the regular reviews of the ritual. Experiment with different rewards and reminders to separate the habit from your daily routine.

Develop Habits That Energize You

What does a gardener do when he sees the leaves of a plant wilting or drooping? He waters it. What do you do when you see the fuel indicator of your car dipping? You fill it up with gas. You see a sign or symptom and respond to it in the required manner. Similarly, if your life is not turning out the way you expect it to, then, this is a sure sign that you need to take action. You need to develop habits that will energize you. These will also bring about results for which you will be thankful in the future. Brushing your teeth once is not enough. You need to do it regularly in order to prevent your teeth and gums from getting damaged. What are the benefits or the results? The instant result is a perfect set of teeth and a confident smile. There are many others: your dental bills become smaller; a confident smile enhances your social standing; you enjoy your food more than someone who has a bad set of teeth; and you spend fewer sleepless nights because of toothache.

Do you see how a simple habit such as brushing your teeth regularly can have a huge impact on your life? There are many such simple yet potentially life-enhancing, life-empowering and life-energizing habits that you can develop. Adopt these habits now, and you will start seeing the change in your life. That's why they are called power habits. They empower you to change your life for the better.

1. Get up early every day
2. Make daily plans
3. Write a daily journal
4. Read every day

5. Tidy up or organize every week
6. Save money every month
7. Go to a new place every year
8. Sit in silence every morning
9. Take a break every hour
10. Stop looking at the clock every few minutes

That's a very effective list of power habits. They probably don't sound as profound as the list of habits you might have come across elsewhere. This might not be the best list. However, what matters is that it is easy to start with and is effective. This means it yields results.

Why are these habits easier? They are simple and straightforward. They are easy to understand. For instance, you don't need an explanation for any of them. If you are told to start a habit which exhorts you to 'think win-win', you will probably have to ponder to figure out what it really means. Writing a daily journal or saving some money every month are such simple things that you can literally start doing them right away.

While this list is simple and easy to follow, it is important to understand why and how it works. Remember the reward–reminder–routine method of introducing a habit? We'll use this method to understand why and how these habits have the potential to empower our lives.

Get Up Early Every Day

We have already seen, in the beginning of this chapter, the disadvantages of not getting up early. You might have experienced this in your own life as well, when being late threw your entire day or schedule out of gear. The main reward for or advantage of getting up early is that you are in control of your schedule. Your chances of success increase if you have more time.

It's a very simple concept. If you are early, you can get ahead of the rest. The first one in a queue gets the ticket before everyone else does. He or she gets a seat in a bus, whereas the last one might miss the bus. When you get up early, you set the tone for the rest of the day. You have enough time to plan your activities. You also set the pace because you don't have to hurry through things. You are relaxed, less stressed and therefore appear more confident and in control of each situation. Though it sounds very easy, most people don't do it because it is so obvious. They would rather do something complicated than something simple.

Many people thrive on the adrenaline rush that they get when they don't have enough time. It's the same reason why some people put off doing a task till the last minute. When a deadline looms, they feel a sense of urgency and they ignore everything else to focus on the task. The truth is that productive people, who actually produce results without appearing busy all the time, are usually early risers.

We have already seen how a simple scheduling system can serve as a reminder to get up early. You go to bed early and wake up early when the alarm goes off. However, how early is early is another matter altogether. For some people, getting up before the sun rises is early. For others, getting up just when the clock shows double digits is early enough.

Whatever your definition of early is, it is important to get a good night's rest before you start the day. This means that if you go to bed at midnight, it is not practical to get up at sunrise.

Even if you manage to, you will be groggy and unproductive. You need to make small changes to develop this habit.

What time do you currently wake up? What time do you think you should actually wake up? If you have to wake up at such-and-such a time, then, when should you go to sleep? How many hours of sleep do you usually need? Every individual has different sleep patterns. It differs according to age, the level of physical activities you undertake, your diet, your geographical location, the season and other factors.

You need to identify your optimal sleep requirement. Decide when it is early enough to get up to go through your day at a comfortable pace, and then count backwards to arrive at the right time for going to bed. This way, you can successfully inculcate the habit of getting up early. Just getting up half an hour earlier than your current time can make a huge difference in your day. A lot of successful people have one thing in common: they wake up early.

If you are a restaurateur or an editor of a newspaper, then, obviously your day begins later than other people and only you know what you can call early. The point is to make an early start, so that you don't rush through your schedule or play catch-up with your tasks.

Make Daily Plans

Almost everyone uses a smartphone or a personal computer nowadays. And yet, most people don't even know that they have a calendar on their devices. The rewards for or advantages of planning your day in advance affect every aspect of your day and life. When you plan your day, you are less likely to forget or miss any important tasks. Planning boosts your productivity. When you plan, you also learn to prioritize your tasks and eliminate activities that waste your time. If your daily plan includes five activities, and if you are still on task number two in the afternoon, you know that you cannot waste time on any extra tasks.

Through planning you also learn how to delegate and not undertake tasks if you are running behind schedule. Let's say you plan to produce twenty units on a particular day. You realize that it takes you nearly three hours to produce five. This means that you cannot produce the remaining fifteen units on your own unless you work overtime. So, it is better to delegate or seek assistance from another person, or more than one person, to help you finish the remaining units.

Sometimes, tasks turn up unexpectedly. You might be asked to run an errand or do something that is not part of your daily plan. Now if you have a schedule, you can easily decide whether you can take on this extra chore and still manage to complete your planned tasks, or whether you should decline the request. Making a daily plan is very simple. You make a 'things-to-do' list and keep it visible at all times. The old-school way of doing this is to write down your list on a pad or piece of paper and stick it on your desk.

However, technology has made this even easier. You can use the calendar on your smartphone or PC. After you have made a list of things to do, you can either number them or rewrite them in the order of importance or priority. This way, even if you have a long list of things and you manage to do only half of them, you will have done the important ones first. Even better, keep your list short. To do this, first delegate the tasks that are at the bottom of your list. Do not try to cram the list with too many things. Give yourself room to breathe or room for extra time because some tasks take more time than you estimate.

Let's say you schedule two meetings, one after the other. If these two meetings are to take place at different venues, then, you need to factor in the travel time between the two locations.

Even if you plan ahead, you might get late for the second meeting due to unexpected factors such as traffic or something else. Space your tasks, so that they don't encroach on the next one and create a domino effect. Plan your day the previous night. This way, you will wake up fresh and ready to start your day because you have already done the planning.

Write a Daily Journal

How is writing a journal different from making a daily plan? You make a plan *before* you start doing the things you want to do. You write a journal *after* you have completed those tasks. Keeping a journal is like saying your prayers. It helps you review your actions, reflect on your day and be grateful for the opportunities you have.

The benefits of writing a journal go beyond your daily routine. The journal helps you review and revise your plan of action, appreciate your achievements, realize and correct your mistakes, and gives you new ideas by clarifying your thoughts.

You need to make the process easy in order to make it into a habit. You can do this by making your journal accessible. Whether you write it on your smartphone, PC, or in a notebook, it is important to keep it in a place where you can access it any time.

Most people prefer to make entries in their journal at the end of the day, because that is when they can review and reflect on the day's activities. Some people write in their journal all through the day, whenever inspiration strikes or they get a thought or an idea, as they are worried that they might forget it if they don't write it down immediately.

Most smartphones and other devices such as tablets now come with apps that make it easier to write things down. If you prefer to carry a pocket notebook and a pen, do so by all means. There are people who prefer to record their thoughts on a personal digital recorder.

To strengthen the journal habit and to remind yourself of the rewards that it will eventually reap, set aside one day of the week to read through and review your journal. You can set a digital reminder on your phone or PC to do this. Reading your own thoughts and ideas can be refreshing, as it opens your mind to the huge potential that you possess.

You don't have to write a lot. Write down your thoughts in short, bullet points. If you make it look like a chore, it will become difficult for you to turn it into a habit.

Don't edit or rewrite what you have written in your journal. It is not supposed to be an example of elegant or eloquent writing. It is meant to be a recording of your thoughts and ideas. It is a road map of your thoughts. It is only for your eyes, and it need not make sense to anyone else but you.

Writing a journal and making daily plans go hand in hand. They are interconnected and one habit helps or reinforces the other. Once writing a daily journal becomes a part of your routine, and you realize how easy and beneficial it is, you will wonder why you had never thought of doing it before.

Read Every Day

Most people have the habit of reading a newspaper every day. Why do we read the newspaper? It is to inform, entertain and educate ourselves on what's happening around the world, isn't it? Our opinions about love, hope, honour, faith, culture, traditions, politics and society are all shaped by what we read. In fact, our moral fibre is defined by what we read—whether it is a storybook, a novel, a self-help book, a book on religion or the scriptures, a memoir or a biography. The books we read shape our world view. Apart from the wealth of information that we gain, it also sharpens our cognitive abilities. After all, reading is one of those qualities that sets us humans apart as the most intelligent species on earth.

The rewards for reading daily are numerous. Research shows that people who read regularly are less stressed, have a sharper memory and are better at concentrating and focusing on tasks. Reading also prevents the brain from succumbing to deterioration caused by ageing. Needless to say, people who read regularly have a better vocabulary, are good communicators and are empathetic towards other people's situations.

Having a book within your reach is the best way to remind yourself to read. Carrying a book with you has never been easier. You can carry thousands of e-books on an e-book reader or an app on a tablet device or smartphone. You can listen to audiobooks. Whether you are commuting to work or waiting for an appointment, technology has made it possible for you to access books any time, anywhere.

Read something that interests and inspires you. You don't have to read something just because it is on a bestseller list or because everyone else is reading it. As I have mentioned earlier, you can even stop reading something midway if you don't like or enjoy it. That's one of the benefits of an e-reader. You are not stuck with just one book, which is usually the case if you are carrying a paperback edition. You can always close a book if you find it boring and open another one on your e-reader.

You will immediately see changes in your personality when you start reading daily. You will be more reflective and open to new ideas and changes than before. You will begin to see beyond the immediate. An open mind and the ability to look ahead, into the future, is one of the greatest rewards for cultivating the habit of reading every day.

Tidy Up or Organize Every Week

There is a character of a detective in a popular series of mystery novels who starts cleaning up her office or desk whenever she gets stuck while solving a case and does not have any serious leads. Organizing things or tidying up the place helps her relax and put her thoughts in order. Invariably, she comes up with a brilliant idea while tidying up, which usually helps her crack a difficult case.

Although this character is fictional, it has been proved that the act of organizing things and tidying benefits a person's physical, mental and emotional well-being. In many Eastern traditions, originating in Japan and China, it is believed that the way things are arranged can affect the productivity of the people working within that space.

You might not have witnessed in person a surgery or operation in progress, but I am sure you have seen one on TV. Have you noticed how every tool a surgeon needs is laid out in an orderly manner? Why? So that the surgeon does not have to waste time rummaging through a set of instruments to find the right one because time is of the essence in a surgical procedure.

When you have a messy desk or office, you spend more time searching for things than doing actual work. How many times have you written a phone number or an address on a piece of paper and been unable to find it when you needed it? How many times have you rummaged in your pockets or bag to look for something and been unable to find it? How many times have you seen people emptying their pockets or bags to look for something? It is not a pleasant sight; moreover, it is a waste of precious time.

Tidy up your surroundings and your life will become simpler and more pleasant. It will help your mental faculties function better. Have you noticed how dance studios are usually free of clutter and well organized? That's because dancers need a clear and clean space to move around in without bumping into things.

Try this simple test. Go into a noisy nightclub, and try to talk to someone. Do you see how the environment does not let you communicate? Now step outside and go for a walk with the same person in a park. Try to have the same conversation you were trying to have inside the nightclub. You will notice how easy it is, even though it had appeared difficult earlier. Your environment affects your performance. Take care of your environment and you will become more productive.

Set aside a few hours on a particular day every week to tidy up your workplace or your desk or your office. You will discover that cleaning up or organizing is surprisingly rewarding. It calms your mind, motivates and inspires you. People who are successful have a clear and sharp idea of what they want in life.

This mindset mirrors the environment they inhabit. **Being mentally strong automatically ensures that you declutter your life. I have helped over 6,00,000 people organize their mind and their life using breakthrough systems that I have created. Check them out on www.wherewillyoubein5years.com.** Observe professionals who are extremely good at what they do, and you will notice that they all keep their workplace organized; it is a common contributor to their excellence.

Whether they are chefs or surgeons, carpenters or gardeners, people who are good at what they do usually keep their tools cleaned and organized. If you want to be good at what you do, make it a habit to tidy up and organize your space once a week.

Clearing your surroundings of clutter also helps you clear the clutter in your mind. Organizing helps to get rid of unnecessary things. If you haven't been using a tool or an item for more than six months, then, you should seriously think about getting rid of it.

Save Money Every Month

There are many people I know, and I am sure you do too, who live from one pay cheque to another. That is, they have literally no money to spare after paying their bills, and saving money is out of the question. In fact, after paying EMIs for loans and credit card bills, they can't even think about saving.

Are you in such a situation? Even if you are, don't worry because your situation is not entirely hopeless. There are many stories of people who, after amassing debts amounting to hundreds and millions of dollars, regained control over their finances, and now live debt-free lives. How did they come back from the brink of a financial disaster? As J.D. Roth, author of the blog getrichslowly.org, says, 'Money is more about the mind than it is about the math.' You only have to make up your mind about the kind of life you wish to live. Do you wish to live like a billionaire on borrowed money when you know deep down in your heart that you are not really entitled to this lifestyle? Or do you wish to live with what you have and be happy rather than borrow and incur debts which will make you unhappy?

It's not difficult to stay debt-free and save money. Don't spend more than you make. In fact, set aside a small percentage of the money you make every month, and it will grow over a period of time. Even a person with a basic understanding of numbers and mathematics will be able to grasp this concept. Why then do people find it so difficult to follow this sound financial advice?

People who choose to spend their money through credit cards and loans even before they earn it don't understand this logical explanation. They don't have the mental discipline to control their spending and to cultivate the saving habit. This prevents them from becoming rich or wealthy.

When I was growing up, I used to find it fascinating to visit houses in our neighbourhood that had a 'For Sale' board. I used to call up the real estate agent to take a tour of the house. A lot of them would try to turn me away after they realized that I was only a child. I would tell them that my parents would soon show up, and by the time they wised up, I would have seen all that I needed to.

What was I doing? I was putting myself in the shoes of the people who owned big houses to see how it felt. It was just a child aping grown-ups. However, the point was that only for a few moments, I was able to experience the joy of living in a big house, and I did this without spending any money or running into debt.

To live like a rich person, you need to think like a rich person. Rich people don't spend money they can't afford to. They spend money they can spare. How did they get to that position? They saved enough and for a long time, so that they didn't have to worry about saving or spending in the future.

That's the main reward for saving money every month. You won't have to worry about money ever again if you start saving every month and make it into a habit. How do you develop this habit?

Let's look at some tips and techniques that smart people employ to save money. The first step is to keep track of your expenses. Most people usually focus on increasing their income and ignore their expenses. While it is important to increase your income by being more productive at your job or by increasing your profit margins, you can't save until you examine and eliminate unnecessary expenses. You can reduce your spending by keeping track of your expenses.

The next step is to stop spending on things before you can afford them. Credit cards have made it easy for people to spend even when they don't have the money. Most people are under the illusion that credit cards are a magic ticket to possessions, and they don't really have to pay for them. They are wrong. Credit cards only make transactions easy. They can't produce money out of thin air. Sooner or later, you have to pay back the money you have spent using a credit card. You will have to spend more by way of penalties and fines if you fail to make these payments on time. Now, why would anyone in their right mind delay making credit card payments when they know this?

Again, it's not that they don't understand the logic, they lack mental discipline.

Try this simple exercise. Take out the credit cards from your wallet and put them away in a locker. Pretend that all you have is the cash in your wallet. You will be surprised at how simple and easy it is to do this. Also, you won't buy things that you would otherwise have bought without thinking twice.

The third step to remind yourself to save money is to take the decision out of your hands. If you get your monthly pay in a bank account, then, ask your bank to transfer a fixed percentage of your earnings to a savings account with a lock-in period. This means that you won't have access to the money that will get deducted from your salary every month and transferred to your savings account. The money will start earning interest and accumulate over a period of time.

You are not only developing a habit without much effort, you are also increasing your income every month with the interest it earns. That's right. Saving every month is a very easy habit to inculcate.

Go to a New Place Every Year

Travel literally broadens yours horizons. You will not only learn to appreciate different cultures, but you will also start acknowledging the importance of your own. Travel does not necessarily mean that you have to get an entry-and-exit stamp on your passport. Just going to a neighbouring town or city can be an enthralling experience as well.

You don't even have to step outside your town or district for that matter. Just go to the local tourist office or visit their website and you will be astonished to find out how many interesting places there are all around you which you haven't seen yet. Whether it's a museum or an art gallery, an ancient monument or a lakeside resort, get out of your comfort zone, your home, and spend some time in a new environment.

Going to a new place will refresh your mind and enable you to see things in a new perspective. Many people use the excuse of not having enough money to travel the world. What they don't realize is that they have enough money to go and see the sunrise from a nearby peak or watch the birds in a sanctuary in their own town. But they choose not to do so and, instead, hanker to visit a monument whose pictures they have seen in a travel brochure.

First, travel to places you can go to, and you will soon realize that you can go wherever you want if you have the will. To get the will, you first need to develop the habit of travelling. Once you start looking, you will discover plenty of great spots nearby that won't cost you the earth. Travelling to these places will do you a power of good, and you will come back to your daily routine relaxed, refreshed and rejuvenated. Taking a holiday, at least once every year, is in itself a reward.

To remind yourself, you just need to make a list of places you want to visit and then put a date or a year next to each of them. There, right there, is your travel schedule for the next few years.

Sit in Silence Every Morning

Sitting in silence helps relieve stress and makes a person mentally and emotionally stronger. Recent research even suggests that sitting in silence can build up stamina, strengthen muscles, and improve concentration. You don't really have to believe in any of these supposed rewards to turn this into a habit. You just have to try it, not once but many times.

However, sitting in silence is not easy. I once overheard a woman telling her woman friend, 'He tells me that I have a blank mind. How is that even possible?' To this, her companion replied, 'How can that be? Your mind is filled with thoughts. Everyone's mind is filled with thoughts all the time. The role of the mind is to be filled with thoughts and not be blank. No one can have a blank mind. Well, not unless you are sitting in silence.'

There you go. Though it's an odd idea, it is very accurate. To sit in silence is to empty your mind of thoughts, and one of the reasons why we don't want to practise this is because we are afraid of letting our thoughts go. I think, at least subconsciously, we know that by sitting in silence we can alter the state of our mind. We can turn a hubbub of activity, thoughts and emotions, into something calm and peaceful, something that is not like the mind at all.

Making your mind calm and peaceful is almost like making a child sit still for a certain period of time. It can't. It's not in its nature to do so. It's difficult, but not completely impossible.

You won't understand why or how sitting in silence works until you try it. The thing is that you will not be able to master it, ever. Now, this may sound very discouraging, but actually that's the best way to approach it. If someone tells you that they sit in silence every morning, what they are actually telling you is that they try to do it. That's correct. Every morning they try and fail, but that's okay because sitting in silence is all about trying and not succeeding. In fact, if you master the art of sitting in silence, you will achieve what very few people have. It's called a 'power state'. So, don't worry about actually sitting in silence every morning. Just try doing it and you'll be fine.

Why morning and not evening?. Well, you can do it at any time of the day, but, as we have seen earlier, doing a task at a particular time is one of the best ways to turn it into a habit. Besides, mornings are the best time to meditate because your mind is in its most relaxed state after a good night's rest. It is more difficult to sit in silence during the day when your mind is swirling with thoughts and emotions. To remind yourself to sit in silence every morning, you can apply these simple yet powerful techniques:

- **Make a commitment**: Commit to two minutes of silence to start with. It's important to start small. Don't be ambitious. In fact, you will notice that those two minutes of silence are as beneficial as doing it for a longer time. Remember, quality matters and not quantity.

- **Make room for silence**: You need to find a quiet and peaceful spot. It can be a corner in your home or a place outdoors, on your terrace or on the beach. Finding a quiet place is important, and you will realize that it is easier to find a quiet place in the morning than at any other time of the day.

- **Pretend**: That's right. Sit down in a comfortable position, close your eyes and observe your breathing. Stay like this and pretend that you are meditating. Remember the exercise about not thinking of the red car in Chapter 4? Apply the same techniques. Very soon you will find that by pretending to do it, you are actually doing it or trying to do it.

When you sit in silence every morning or you try to, you will discover the hidden reserves of strength that lie deep within you. You will discover a stronger person within you; a person who is not quick to get angry, who does not get stressed very easily, who does not give up on things, and whose mind can achieve unattainable heights of insight. You will be amazed at the change your body and mind experience by spending just two minutes every morning. Don't you think it's worth trying?

Take a Break Every Hour

Did you know that you can be more productive if you work for a shorter period of time? Though most people claim to work six to eight hours a day, they are actually productive only for about three to four hours. That is, they need to spend only three to four hours to achieve that day's target. So, why do they end up working for eight hours every day?

It's a question that both individuals and corporations need to ask themselves. What do most people who sit at desks do all day? Are they actually working or are they checking their e-mails or browsing the web or checking posts on social networking websites?

Earlier in the chapter, we figured that the best way to make meditation a habit is by pretending. This is actually what most people do when they seem to be engrossed in work. They are pretending to work and not actually working.

Instead of checking your inbox every few minutes or every time a pop-up window announces the arrival of a new e-mail, why don't you shut down your personal e-mail app or sign out of it? Just check your e-mails once a day and be done with it. This is exactly what Timothy Ferriss did. He checked his e-mails only once a day. That's how he found the time to write the bestseller, *The 4-Hour Workweek*.

'Being busy is a form of laziness,' says Ferriss. Doing things that have no benefits, such as checking your e-mail or continuing to work or trying to when your heart is not in it or when your mind cannot concentrate, is pointless. It is a form of laziness to avoid doing actual, productive work. To be really productive, you need to know when to stop. Take a break every hour, for just five to ten minutes or so, and you will notice the difference. You will feel more energized and refreshed, and you will be able get back to your work with renewed enthusiasm and energy.

How do you remind yourself to take a break every hour? Well, since most of us work on a computer, sitting at a desk, it is easy. You just have to set hourly reminders on your computer. You can even set an alarm for every hour on your smartphone or PC.

There are also many apps on your smartphone or tablet which help you do this. Once the alarm goes off, stop doing whatever you are at that moment and go for a walk. Do just that. Get up and go for a walk. Drink a glass of water. Go out on the balcony and get some fresh air. What's the point of this? It'll make you more productive and you will stay healthier too. How is that? Research says that sitting for too long is not good for you. In fact, they say sitting is the new smoking. Yes, sitting in one position for too long, especially for more than an hour can be very unhealthy. It causes physical and mental inertia. When you take a break every hour, you actually recharge your mental faculties and facilitate blood circulation in your legs and brain.

If you think taking a break every hour is a new and revolutionary idea, you are mistaken. In the 1980s, an entrepreneur called Francesco Cirillo developed what became famous as the Pomodoro Technique. He used a kitchen timer, shaped like a tomato, to time his work for twenty-five minutes, after which he would take a break. The technique not only helped him get more work done but also produced better results. Pomodoro, Italian for tomato, was the term he used to define each stretch of activity, so named after the tomato-shaped timer that he used.

So, taking a break every hour is not that big a deal. In fact, to develop this habit, you can start with taking breaks every hour and then take more frequent ones, every half an hour, like Cirillo did. When you get back from your break, you will notice the difference in how you feel and how much more work you are able to complete in a shorter period of time. This habit will reward you with increased productivity, and keep you healthier.

Stop Looking at the Clock Every Few Minutes

If the person you are talking to or having coffee with starts looking at his or her watch every few minutes, what does it imply? That the person is not interested in what you are saying or that what you are saying is too boring to hold that person's interest. This is what happens when we are distracted. When you are doing one thing but thinking of something else—probably the thing you have to do next—you tend to look at the time every few minutes. You do the same thing when you are late for something.

Imagine this. You are waiting for a train and it is past its scheduled arrival time. You keep looking at the time every few minutes. What are you achieving? Nothing. Do you think the train will arrive sooner if you keep looking at the time? No. Do you want to be relaxed and at ease while working or do you want to be stressed and harried? People claim that they perform better under pressure, but to create a false sense of pressure is foolish.

Instead of wasting your time looking at the clock, get on with your work. Time won't slow down if you keep looking at it. You will only get more stressed. One day, this pressure will blow up and land you in the emergency room.

How can you break this habit? The key to this lies in the earlier habit. When you set reminders for every hour to take a break, you don't have to watch the clock because the clock is watching you.

It Just Takes a Little Effort

By now you have probably come to the conclusion that most of the power habits, if not all, appear to be quite easy and are therefore insignificant. How can you change your life by doing something so small and insignificant? Well, most things that appear small are not necessarily insignificant. In fact, it's the small things that matter the most. This is what the bakers in a little town failed to understand and, therefore, could not draw customers the way one of them did.

This baker, named Ben, made the best bread in town. While the other bakers concentrated on adding more variety to their fare, such as cakes and pastries, Ben only made bread which was the best in town and got sold out before noon.

The other bakers did business only when Ben ran out of bread. They were fascinated by the quality of his bread and asked him what the secret was. Ben smiled and said, 'I just do it the way I've always done it. Perhaps I knead the dough longer than you do.'

So, the other bakers went back and kneaded their dough longer than usual. Their bread was still not as good as Ben's. 'Perhaps, I smile a lot at my customers, and that's why they buy my bread?' said Ben. The other bakers tried and failed. 'Is it the ingredients?' asked one of the bakers. 'Tell us where you buy the flour, the sugar, the milk, and so on.' Ben told them from where he bought his supplies. The other bakers still could not match the quality of his bread. 'Perhaps, it's the honey. I add a drop to the dough while kneading it,' said Ben. So the other bakers went back and added honey. Still the customers stood in line for Ben's bread. The other bakers gave up. They decided that it was their fate to sell bread to people who came empty-handed from Ben's bakery.

Then one day, Ben ran out of honey, so he went to one of the other bakeries to borrow some. The other baker was kneading his dough. So Ben waited, and while waiting he watched him at work. Suddenly Ben said, 'You don't have to add more than a drop of honey. You are adding too much.' 'How can just a little more than a drop make any difference?' said the baker as he generously added honey to the dough. Ben shrugged and said,

'Just a little is all it takes, as far as I know, to make something or break something.'

Sometimes, a little more effort can take you faster towards your goals, sometimes a little less hesitation can lead you to success. Ultimately, it is the choice you make.

8

How You Choose to Live
Is Up To You

'In any moment of decision, the best thing you can do is the right thing. The worst thing you can do is nothing.'

— Theodore Roosevelt

One day, a wise man visited a village. Most of the villagers came to meet with him and seek his advice. They not only brought gifts for him, but also brought their burdens, worries, problems that they could not solve, and the doubts in their minds. After meeting with the wise man, they all returned home, satisfied. Soon, everyone was praising his limitless wisdom.

Two friends, Ramesh and Sohan, who lived in the village, wanted to see for themselves what the hullabaloo was all about. So they approached the wise man.

The wise man met with each person in private to focus on his/her problems without any distractions. So Ramesh met the wise man first, followed by Sohan. On their way back home, Ramesh asked, 'So, what do you think? Is he really wise?'

Sohan replied, 'I don't know. I thought I would be the one asking him questions. That's not what happened though. I felt like I had nothing much to say. He asked most of the questions.' Ramesh laughed and said, 'You know what? I feel exactly the same way. He made me feel like I knew more than him. I felt wiser in his presence.'

'Perhaps, that's the reason they call him wise. Did he give you anything?' asked Sohan.

'No,' replied Ramesh. 'Why? Did he give you something?'

'No.'

In truth, both the friends were lying to each other. They had both received the same gift from the wise man. It was a string of beads. The wise man had given both of them exactly the same advice. 'Here, take this but I have to warn you. Though it is just an ordinary string of beads, in your hands it can acquire the power to influence your perception of life. Keep it close to you at all times. Count the beads when you are doing nothing, and you will discover the power they have.'

Sohan thought it was something between him and the wise man, so he didn't tell his friend about the string of beads. Ramesh felt the same way.

A few years passed. The wise man returned to the village. People flocked to see him again. Ramesh and Sohan also went to meet with him.

This time Sohan went first. The wise man asked him, 'So, do you still have the string of beads I gave you?' Sohan scratched his head, looked here and there, and then said sheepishly, 'I am sorry, but I lost them.'

'Never mind,' said the wise man with a smile. 'I guess they served their purpose then.'

'Oh! So, you are not angry that I lost them? I thought you would be upset!'

'Well, obviously, they were not that important to you. Were they?'

Sohan smiled. 'To tell you the truth, I thought they were just baubles.' They talked about other things for a while, and then Sohan took his leave.

Then it was Ramesh's turn. As soon as he entered the room, he took out the string of beads and gave it back to the wise man. 'Here, I don't want these. They are useless. They are worry beads,' said Ramesh.

'What do you mean by worry beads?' asked the wise man.

'Every time I hold them in my hand and count, I can think of nothing else but my worries. I don't think they are of any help.'

The wise man took the string and opened a cloth bag to put it in.

'Wait!' said Ramesh. 'You have a whole bag of worry beads? What do you do with so many of them?'

'I give them to people, and sometimes, like you, they give them back to me.'

The wise man opened the cloth bag so that Ramesh could take a good look at his collection of strings of beads. There were at least twenty to thirty of them of different colours and sizes.

'Go ahead. You can touch them and hold them,' said the wise man. 'You will get a glimpse of the lives of other people.'

Ramesh hesitated and then picked up one. As soon as he touched it, he had a vision of sickness and poverty. He dropped it back into the bag and picked up another. This time, a feeling of hatred and discontent flashed through his mind. He dropped the string and took another one. He felt lonely and sad as soon as he held it in his hands. He dropped it back, and looked at the wise man in wonder. 'Why do you carry all those with you?'

'I take them back from people who don't want them,' said the wise man. 'When I gave them to people, they were just ordinary strings of beads. They became worry beads, as you call them, in the hands of people who had worries or problems in their lives.'

'So, will my worries go away now that I have given the beads back to you?' asked Ramesh.

'No, your worries are yours. You created them yourself. Only you can get rid of them,' said the wise man. 'Other people have their own sets of worries, as you have already seen. Do you want to exchange your worries for theirs?'

'No,' said Ramesh, immediately. 'I guess I am better off than the others who have returned their strings.'

The wise man smiled. 'So, would you like to talk about something else other than your worries?'

Four Steps to Create an Extraordinary Life

1.   You Are Happy When 'You' Make the Choice

When Ramesh picked up the other worry beads from the cloth bag, he understood that his worries were small and insignificant compared to what others had. He realized he was lucky in many ways. He was healthy and was doing quite well for himself. He had inherited his father's business, and it was thriving. He had a loving family, a beautiful wife and two wonderful children. He saw that he had been so busy focusing on his worries that he had forgotten to count his blessings.

So, what was he worried about? Well, this and that. Once in a while he felt that he would have done better in his business had he been smarter. At other times, he felt that he would have been happier if he had gone and learnt a trade like Sohan. To a friend, who knew both Ramesh and Sohan, their lives seemed perfect. Well, Sohan's house was not as big as Ramesh's, but he seemed happy where he was. They were still friends and went to each other's house on occasions like birthdays, anniversaries or festivals. Their families celebrated together and shared their joys and sorrows. So, why did Ramesh envy Sohan? Well, Sohan could have been a farmer just like his father, but he decided not to. Instead, he chose carpentry and learnt to work with wood. Sohan's father was disappointed. Sohan was the eldest son, and by tradition he would have inherited the farm. But since he was not interested, his younger brother did.

When we see a king, we envy him. Why? We think he has all the riches and power. We don't stop to think whether the king had even wanted to be a king or not. Had he had a choice? In a monarchy, the eldest son or the only son of the king has to take over the throne. What if the prince doesn't want the crown when he grows up? What if he wants to do something else with his life?

He can't, because he has no choice but to be the king. You, on the other hand, have a choice. You can be whoever you want to be. So, make that choice wisely. The choices you make in your life will define your happiness.

In a democracy, a person chooses to be a leader, and hence contests the position. The president of a state chooses the position because he/she thinks that they can be a leader, and most people agree with them. Life becomes easy when you make the right choices and accept and agree with the choices that you have made. You are happy because you are doing what you want to do, and you are living your life on your own terms.

Ramesh was concentrating on his failures instead of counting his blessings. This was because he wasn't happy with the choices he had made. It made him focus more on his worries than on his blessings. Sohan, on the other hand, was satisfied because he had made a choice to lead his life the way he wanted to.

We often seek answers in books or from people who we think know better than us. Many a time, the answer is right under our noses or sometimes within us.

Have you seen children playing in a playground? They don't go there after reading an instruction manual on 'How to Have Fun'. They just go and play. They instinctively know how to play and enjoy themselves. We should adopt their attitude; we should follow our heart just as they do.

2.   Trust Your Instinct to Succeed

Everyone has the potential to succeed. People who achieve success are those who discover this potential within them. You don't need someone to tell you how to enjoy your life. You need to listen to your heart. You need to do what you think is right.

Do you know why some people are miserable even though they seem to have everything? That is because they have everything they don't want and don't have the things they want.

You may be good at your job as a designer, but if you think that selling cars might be more exciting then, you will be miserable and unhappy unless you try it. You may suck at selling cars or may be good at it. You will never know unless you try it. Every person has his or her own qualities which are unique to them, just like their fingerprints. You might succeed in some aspects of your life. There might be room for improvement in the others.

Where there is light, there are shadows. When you look at your life, look at the advantages. Don't look only at the disadvantages and worry about them. There is no point focusing on your worries if you are not going to do anything about them. If you can change your life for the better and get rid of your worries, do it. If you can't, then, what's the point of worrying about something which you cannot change or don't have the power to change? Take the good aspects of your life and capitalize on them. Take the ones you are not happy with and try to improve on them.

Let's say, you have a natural talent for cooking. You can turn it into your profession and become a chef. You can open a restaurant. On the other hand, you probably lack accounting and management skills. So, what do you do? You hire a manager and an accountant.

Also, you should not concentrate only on one part of your life, such as your health or your relationships, and make that the most important aspect of your life. Remember the wheel of life? You need to balance and focus on each aspect equally. The money you make or the things you own are just a part of your life. There are other things equally important such as your work, your family and your learning curve.

Similarly, a small part of one aspect of your life, such as your health, should not influence the whole of it. I have a friend who has asthma but he is also a great athlete. He did not let a physical handicap come in the way of his desire to become an athlete.

* * *

One of my friends is a multimillionaire but prefers to live in a small apartment even though he can easily afford to live in a mansion. He did not do what many do with their money—build a big house to showcase their wealth. Instead, he owns a dozen small apartments in different cities across the world. He doesn't have to worry about hotel bookings when he visits these cities because he's got an apartment in each one of them.

These are people who know what they want and who live their life on their own terms. These people march to a different tune and not the popular one. They trust their own instinct to succeed.

* * *

A friend's mother was diagnosed with cancer at a very late stage in the disease. One of the doctors told the family that they could try chemotherapy and other treatments, but the chances of the person surviving were low. The family wanted a second opinion. So they consulted another doctor, who said that though her cancer was incurable, it was treatable. The family wanted to know what he meant by that. He said that they could prolong the patient's life by a few months by treating her. The family asked the person who was suffering what she wanted to do. My friend's mother replied, 'I want to spend the rest of my life living. I don't want to spend it trying not to die.'

They had two choices. They could consider the option of treating her and spend a lot of money to make the rest of her life miserable. The other option was to let her spend the rest of her life doing what she wanted.

My friend's mother chose the latter; she did not want to spend the rest of her life in a hospital. She wanted to paint. She used to paint when she was young. Then, life took over, and she didn't have time to pursue this hobby. She got married and became busy raising her children. Now that she knew she was going to die, she wanted to paint again. Despite protests from her family members, she got herself discharged from the hospital, bought brushes, canvases and paints, and spent her remaining days doing what she liked.

Today, when I visit the family and look at the paintings in their living room, I see a testament to the will of a strong woman, a woman who did not let a disease defeat her. I still remember what she said to her family when she came to know that she was going to die: 'I made this choice and I am happy I made it. I prefer to live life on my own terms rather than fight death when I know I can't win.'

3. Your Actions Define Your Life

Your purpose in life is to discover what you want to do and then do it. Let us take a typical day in your life. On your way back from work, you stop at a shop to buy something. You happen to look out and see a familiar face on the street. Suddenly, you realize you know this person from school, perhaps your childhood sweetheart or best friend. You immediately run out of the shop, and call out your friend's name. He or she turns around and you get talking. After a while, you realize that you haven't picked up the carton of milk and loaf of bread that you were in the process of buying when you saw your old friend. When you go back to the shop, you see that they have closed for the day. That day could be defined as the day you met your friend or the day you forgot to buy bread and milk.

Let's take another example. You are sitting in a café talking to your financial broker on the phone, who has just told you about a deal that could net you a significant amount of money. Suddenly, you see a child running across the street. At the same time, you see a truck coming the same way. You drop your phone and rush across the street to prevent the accident. You hear the screeching of brakes and the smell of burnt rubber as the truck comes to a halt.

This day could be defined as the day you saved a life. Or as the day you lost a good opportunity to make a lot of money. Of course, nothing as dramatic happens in real life most of the time. Yet, you know that you will instinctively do what you think or believe is right.

You wouldn't miss the opportunity to meet a long-lost friend just because you were busy buying a loaf of bread, would you? You wouldn't close your eyes and let someone die just because you were busy making money, would you? You instinctively know what you have to do. You know that your life is not ordinary. Don't get so caught up in the busyness of life that you ignore the opportunities in front of you. At the same time, don't expect dramatic twists of fate to turn your life around. You have to build your life day by day. Every action, no matter how small, counts. **Discover once and for all what shapes your identity to learn how to act; it's a simple technique that I teach. Log on to www.wherewillyoubein5years.com to access my online course, 'Where Will You Be in Five Years', that is free with this book.**

4.   Choose Quality over Quantity Every Time

Success and smartness are often overrated, just as talent and fate are given too much importance. In an experiment conducted at a university, each subject was given two chocolates to choose from. One was an ordinary-sized chocolate, which could be easily consumed in a mouthful, while the other was about four times the size of the first. The subjects would have to take a few bites to eat it. They were also told that both the chocolates tasted the same.

The key difference, however, was not the size but the shape of the chocolates. The smaller one was shaped like a flower. The bigger one was shaped like a cockroach, quite lifelike and repulsive. Surprisingly, a majority of the participants chose the bigger chocolate despite its distasteful appearance. What is even more significant is that all those participants were considered smart and successful. That is, they were well-educated, with postgraduate degrees or doctorates, healthy, married, and earning a steady income. In other words, they were all outstanding citizens with a track record of professional success and good social standing.

A small number of the participants, however, chose the smaller chocolate. In terms of enjoyment and satisfaction, it was found that those who ate the bigger chocolate did not enjoy the experience.

When asked whether they would make the same choice again, given another opportunity, they said that they would choose the smaller chocolate. On the other hand, those who ate the smaller chocolate said that they had enjoyed it and would choose the same again.

Planning is important but nothing happens without taking action. Most people spend their entire lives just planning. If you want to make your next five years the beginning of the best years of your life, then, it's time to take action.

9

Why Actions Are Critical

'Good is the enemy of great.'

— James C. Collins

Now that we have discussed your habits and how to plan your schedule, it's time to understand how to put this into action. In a beehive, there are three types of bees—the queen bee, the drones and the worker bees. The queen bee, of course, rules the hive and lays the eggs. The drones are responsible for reproduction and stay close to the hive. Their sole function is to mate with the queen bee. The worker bees fly from flower to flower, gather nectar and transport it to the beehive, convert it into honey and store it as food for the other inhabitants of the hive. It's an ecosystem, a natural one, which works quite well the way it does.

We can use the beehive as a metaphor to understand how organizations work or how most activities are performed. It's another parallel of the Pareto Principle or the 80/20 rule.

As I had mentioned earlier, this principle says that about 80 per cent of the results that are achieved come from 20 per cent of the actions performed. It also indicates that 80 per cent of an organization's profits actually come from just about 20 per cent of its clients or customers. You can also infer that 80 per cent of the performance comes from about 20 per cent of the employees.

'That's one busy bee,' you say when you see an industrious person. However, it's hard to tell the difference between a drone and a worker bee, especially when they are close to the hive. Drones make the same amount of buzz or noise as the worker bees. Similarly, many people act busy and even manage to fool not just others but also themselves that they are actually doing something worthwhile when they are just looking busy for the sake of it. Similarly, many of us perform certain actions with the notion that doing something is better than doing nothing. It's certainly better than doing nothing, but it is not as good as doing a task that will produce real results. The drones make a lot of buzz, which is merely noise or illusion. They don't make honey. The workers make a lot of buzz as well but they also make honey. Knowing the difference between mere action for the sake of action and the right kind of action or purposeful action makes a person produce substantial and quantifiable results. You need to focus on the actions that produce results. You need to be the worker bee and not the drone. In other words, you need to perform actions that will produce honey.

Acting without Focus Is a Waste of Energy

Thinking before taking action is important. However, don't overthink. Can you walk a tightrope stretched across two tall buildings? No, you can't, and you wouldn't even think about it unless you were an acrobat or a daredevil. Now, what if someone offered you a million dollars to do it? You would consider it, wouldn't you? At least for a brief moment, but then, you would stop and think. You still wouldn't do it, because it is not worth the risk.

You also know that you wouldn't be able to keep your balance, and no amount of money can compensate for doing something for which you are not prepared, or in which you have no talent or practice. Now, what if someone gave you enough time, say a month, to practise tightrope walking ? Would you then consider doing it? At the very least, you would practise keeping balance. You don't know whether you will succeed, but you can try by practising walking a tightrope that is not too high and which has a safety net below.

What if someone were to put a gun to your head and tell you to walk the tightrope? You would have no choice. It's either a bullet or a fatal fall. Now, take the same length of rope and place it on the ground in an open space. Stretch the rope so that it is taut and in a straight line. Can you walk along the straight line that the rope has created on the ground? Of course, you can. You don't even have to think about it, do you?

When we are about to perform an action, sometimes we think about it and sometimes we don't or we don't have to. The actions that we don't have to think about are the ones we are used to performing. They have become habits. You do them automatically, without thinking.

You tend to delay or procrastinate doing the ones for which you have to plan. When you have an important task that you are afraid of performing, you tend to delay it by busying yourself with other unnecessary tasks.

Does this sound familiar? Let's take an example. At work, you know that you have to call a client and ask him or her about the status of a bill or a payment which is due. Instead, you check your e-mails, sharpen your pencils, make coffee, and so on. You do everything else but make that call because you are afraid of the outcome. You finally make that call. However, you get a vague answer. You hang up and tell yourself that you did it.

Yes, you made that call but it did not produce the results you expected it to.

Did you ask when you would get the cheque? Yes, and your client said, soon. Did you ask for a date? No, you didn't. You did an unpleasant task but it was a half-hearted attempt because you were afraid that you would fail, and you did fail because you were afraid.

If you had thought through and prepared for the possible responses, then, you would have known how to perform the task in a much more effective manner. You would have taken control of the call and pinned down a date for the payment.

To Open One Door, Close All the Others

I met Rachna at my 'call of destiny' seminar. A married woman with two children, she was a real go-getter but had lost her confidence after putting on weight. During the seminar, Rachna said that she wanted to lose weight to go to the gym. At first I didn't understand the resolution. How could she get into shape if she didn't have a gym membership in the first place? Then it struck me what she meant. Rachna was afraid to go to the gym. Why? She was scared that other people at the gym would laugh at her because she was out of shape. Then I asked her what she was really afraid of? After some introspection, she admitted that she was merely finding excuses to avoid going to the gym. She knew that if she went to the gym even once, she would have to continue doing so every day, on a regular basis. She was afraid to take that first step. What else was she afraid of? She was afraid that, in spite of all her efforts, she might not be able to lose weight.

Rachna knew that she had let herself grow too fat and become too inactive to get back into shape. She had lulled herself into a state of inaction. She needed a push to break out of her shell.

I asked her to stand with her back against a wall, close her eyes and imagine that she was in a desert. If she went ahead, she might find water. If she went back, she would definitely find water. So, what would she do?

'But I can't go back, can I?' she said. When I didn't reply, Rachna got angry and shouted, 'How can I go back when there is a wall behind me!'

'Exactly,' I said. 'The only way is forward, or you can stay where you are.' The next day, Rachna went to the gym. She didn't care whether people laughed at her. The next year, I heard her laughing at a party. When I asked her what the joke was, she replied, 'What do you do when there's a wall behind you?'

You can plan up to a point but there comes a time when you need to act and take that first step. If the tightrope is too high, lower it. If you are still afraid, put a safety net. If you still can't take that first step, put a wall behind you. Close all doors of escape if you want to move forward, towards success.

Talk to Someone When in Doubt

If you have been putting off something for a while, then, obviously you have doubts about doing it. When you are in two minds about something, it not only affects your thinking but also your performance. It also affects your other actions. As we have seen earlier, you might be doing something just for the sake of keeping yourself busy and not doing that one thing which you know you should do. To put it bluntly, you waste your time in frivolous activities when you should do what is important or essential. When things are not clear in your mind, when you are confused, it helps to talk to someone. When you say it out loud you are actually facing your fears. You are turning the spotlight on those grey doubts to see them clearly.

More often than not, your fears about performing an action are akin to the fears that children have about imaginary monsters that lurk under the bed or in the closet at night. Once you turn on the light or look at your fears in broad daylight, they no longer make you uncomfortable.

In this case, you underline your doubts when you express them to someone. You recognize the fears for what they are, or at least get some advice or guidance from your friend, guide, well-wisher or mentor.

Fear Can Be Used to Motivate

Everyone experiences fear. Even the most experienced athletes are afraid, no matter how much they practise or how motivated they are. Even the most successful performers experience stage fright before a performance. What are we afraid of? Is it failure? Why are we afraid of failing? The explanation for the adrenaline rush that we get when we are about to do something important lies in our brain. To be more precise, it lies in a primitive part of our brain called the amygdala, which is sometimes referred to as the lizard brain. It's a survival instinct from the days when we constantly faced danger.

Soldiers who have gone through a recent combat or war ordeal experience an acute form of this. It's the 'fight or flight' instinct when we sense danger. It's the way a lizard behaves when it is cornered. It can't think because its brain is numb and it sees only two alternatives, survival or death. When we are about to perform an action, our amygdala, the lizard brain, gets activated. Interestingly, the amygdala also gets activated when we experience anger or sexual desire, both of which, like fear, can cause a momentary lapse of reasoning.

Our response in the face of danger is to flee, to move towards safety or to fight. When we are afraid of performing an action, or doing something, our first instinct is to back out. This is the brain's way of seeking safety. The second is to face the situation boldly and overcome it. Feel the fear but don't let it deter you from performing the task. Use your fear to propel you in the right direction. How do you do this? See your fear as a fork in the road. The left turn could lead you in the wrong direction; the right turn could take you to your destination. You can either fail or succeed at a task. The third option is to stay frozen at the crossroads or go back the way you came.

Imagine looking back at the crossroads five years from now. Will you regret not taking the turn or turning your back on an opportunity? Take that turn. Feel scared but still take action. The worst outcome is failure. You will at least know that you tried and, who knows, you might win. **Don't let the fear of failing stop you. Want to know how to change your state to feel powerful? There is a technique which I discuss in my free online course on www.wherewillyoubein5years.com.**

Live in the Moment

When you have decided to do something, stop thinking about it. That's correct, stop thinking and let your mind go blank.

This is how goals are scored and matches are won, how great things are achieved and how an ordinary person finds the energy to do something extraordinary.

At the moment of action, focus all your energy and concentrate on doing it; don't think about doing it or create mental images of yourself doing it. You will reach a state of mind where you won't be aware of anything else but the action that is being performed.

You might think that this is contradictory to what we call 'mindfulness' because the mind is actually absent while performing the task. But in reality the mind is so deeply involved in the task that it becomes one with the body. Psychologist Mihaly Csikszentmihályi called it 'being in the flow'. It has also been referred to as being in the zone.

It is a state of mind where you lose track of time and concentrate on performing a task. You have to be absent from everything else around you to focus on the task on hand. Of course, you don't have to do this for simple tasks such as washing dishes or sharpening a pencil. However, when an action demands intense concentration, being in the flow can enable you to perform it in the best possible manner.

When a footballer kicks a ball which scores a goal, or a chess player checkmates his or her opponent, they are generally in the 'flow'. This state of mind can also be achieved through meditation. Paradoxically, while meditating, a person is not doing anything, but he or she needs to be in this state of mind. So, do all your thinking and planning well before you get down to performing the task. When in action, stop thinking and just do it.

A Masterpiece Is the Result of a Million Mistakes

We often settle for something that is good enough because we are afraid of succeeding. Our mind is afraid of succeeding, just as it is afraid of failure.

The fear of success comes from the fear of future responsibilities that will follow after you succeed. Once you display your ability to rise above the mediocre, everyone expects an above-average or extraordinary performance from you. Your mind is aware of this possibility, and it makes you shirk work that might produce a masterpiece. We often make mistakes because we subconsciously sabotage our own success. How can you prevent yourself from doing this? Make up your mind that you won't give up. Do it with the determination that you are going to keep at it no matter what.

The beach on which you walk is made of grains of sand from a mountain on which you could never have set foot. The building in which you now live was just an architect's vision on a piece of paper in the beginning. Transformations at a great level happen when the mind is able to comprehend what is possible and what can come out of nothing. A blank piece of canvas is transformed into a masterpiece that hangs in an art gallery. A few musical notes produce different emotions in a million hearts. We don't see the many pieces of paper crumpled up and thrown in the dustbin, the many pieces of canvas painted and discarded, the hours spent in anguish and action. Not every action produces success. Some fail, some achieve moderate success.

Will you settle for good when you can achieve great? Will you be content with okay instead of awesome? Will you aim for gold or be happy with silver? The choice is yours. All actions produce results. Consistent and committed actions produce the desired results.

Successful people are also great decision-makers and make the right choices. What makes them achieve success consistently? What makes them have a 'never give up' attitude. Read on . . .

10

The Commitment Contract

'*Make sure every day you do what matters most. When you know what matters most, everything makes sense. When you don't know what matters most, anything makes sense.*'

— Gary Keller

I consider two personal experiences as important turning points in my life. The first one has an action hero in it. The other has an emotional appeal. They both have meaningful lessons that changed my life for the better.

About four years ago, I went from being overweight to fighting fit. I did this in less than three months. I had been overweight for a while, and I knew that I had to get fit and lose weight. It was on my to-do list. I had just not made it a priority. In less than ten weeks, I managed to shed over twelve kilograms. How did I do this? I did it with the help of my friend, the Bollywood action hero and actor, Hrithik Roshan.

I met Hrithik and told him that I wanted to lose weight. He said, 'What would you say if I told you that I have an exercise and diet plan that will help you lose twelve kilograms in ten weeks?' My immediate reaction was doubt but when I saw the look on his face, I knew he meant business. I looked at Hrithik. The man obviously knew what he was talking about. I could see the results right in front of me. He is one of the fittest human beings I know. I said, 'All right. I believe you. I'll do it.' 'What? Really?' Hrithik was a bit taken aback at how easily and quickly I agreed. He said, 'Don't you want to see the fitness plan?' I shrugged and said, 'Of course I want to see it, but I don't have to right now. I mean I don't have to see it to know whether it will work or not.' I could see the confidence in his eyes, and I was more than excited about the plan. I had now committed to losing weight and making it work.

I valued and had respect for our friendship. By committing to the challenge, I had put my respect for this friendship at stake. If I didn't stick to my commitment, I would lose something very valuable—faith, friendship and respect for my word.

I was also putting my reputation as a coach on the line. I was always telling people the importance of putting plans into action. Here was an opportunity for me to walk the talk. If I could not trust my own judgement and ability to transform words into action, then, how could I expect others to trust me?

To his credit, Hrithik had made a foolproof fitness regimen that told me exactly what to eat and what not to, when to eat and how much. With this, he had also prepared a detailed exercise plan. Everything had been worked out in an amazingly detailed manner. I just had to stick to the plan, and I was sure that I would get the desired results at the end of ten weeks. As we all know, the tough part is 'sticking to a plan', but I had worked it out all in my mind about how I was going to stay committed. It worked, and once again I realized the importance of making a commitment. I had to burn 1000 calories per day. It was tough, and whenever I felt weak, I remembered my commitment. I was put on a restricted diet, but I was eating more food than I had ever eaten before, albeit the right kind of food. Whenever I felt like having an ice cream or any of the foods I wasn't allowed to eat, I remembered my commitment. So every day, for ten weeks, I ate five meals a day, burnt 1000 calories and drank a lot of water. The first two weeks were tough, but the result was magical.

* * *

A few years ago, I experienced another turning point. One day, my parents were in a nostalgic mood and started talking about India. It was nothing in particular but generally about the people, the culture, the festivals, history, and so on. At that time, we were living in the UK. I sensed in them a strong attachment, emotional and cultural, to the country of our origin. Their passion was infectious, and I felt a deep desire to visit India and seek a few answers. I was not sure what I had in mind, but I knew it would all become clear at the right moment. When I finally visited India, I immediately knew what I had to do. I made up my mind to establish a business here. I faced a lot of challenges initially, and almost gave up. In moments of despair, I thought of my parents and remembered the fondness with which they had talked about the country, its culture and people. This renewed my commitment and strengthened my determination to succeed.

In less than a year after my first visit to India, I invited my parents to attend an event in India. I didn't tell them then what it was. 'It's a surprise,' I told them. They didn't know what was in store. It was a seminar I was hosting in Mumbai. I wanted to demonstrate to them that I had succeeded in my efforts, and that I had made their dreams come true. Around 2000 people attended that seminar which taught them about their 'millionaire blueprint'. I felt really happy when everyone went up to them at the end of the seminar and congratulated them. I had established links in the country of our origin. The happiness that I saw in my parents' eyes was worth all the effort and challenges I'd faced in setting up the business.

Are You Interested or Are You Committed?

I had long been aware of the fact that I needed to lose weight. I knew I was not eating right or getting enough exercise. I knew I had to make some drastic lifestyle changes. I was 'interested' in making those changes. However, being interested in something is not always enough. You need to be committed to make it happen. Being interested in something is just thinking about it. Being committed is doing something about it.

It all became clear in my mind when I accepted Hrithik's challenge. It acted as a catalyst. It made me commit to a plan. I now had a specific goal. I had always had a goal: to lose weight. But now I had something very specific, which was to lose ten kilograms in ten weeks. There was a clear-cut objective and a time frame in which I had to achieve it.

Also, the fact that there was something important at stake made me stick to the commitment. My friendship with Hrithik and my reputation as a coach are both very important to me. Once I had committed to the fitness plan and diet programme, I knew I had to stay with it. I could not afford to go back on my word. Lastly, I was accountable to my mentor. Throughout those ten weeks, the thought of Hrithik reminded me of my commitment to lose weight.

His commitment to his health and daily fitness routine is legendary. He never misses a meal or a workout session, no matter what. Even during busy shoots, he finds the time to take care of himself. I had a sterling example of determination and discipline right in front of me, and I was inspired, motivated and committed.

Similarly, when I decided to establish a business in India, I was attracted not only by the potential for growth in a new market, or the prospect of tapping into the enormous talent and opportunities that were available. Of course, as in any business venture, these were among the factors of interest. But it was my parents' desire to establish a connection with their homeland that laid the foundation for my commitment. That had been the catalyst and my driving force through the process.

If I had been merely interested in establishing a business, I could have done it anywhere else other than India, and it would have been, perhaps, much easier. My motivation was not merely the profits or growth, it was also fulfilling my parents' dreams and desires. I was 'committed' to give them happiness and satisfaction. I put the respect and devotion I felt for my parents at stake as I had, in my mind, attached failure to disrespect. When we talk about being interested in something, we are expressing a desire to do it. When we say that we are committed to it, we are passionate about it, and want to accomplish it no matter what. When you are merely interested, you give excuses, you procrastinate and eventually lose interest. When you are committed, there is no place for excuses. There is no more thinking and planning, there is only action. You also have a lot to lose if you back out of your commitment. In short, when you are committed, there is no looking back.

Make a Commitment Contract

If you have worked for a company or a client or if you are married, you might be familiar with the term contract. When a person is hired by an organization or an employer, he or she is expected to sign an employment contract. Similarly, when you marry someone, you enter into a contract which in most cases does not really exist on paper, but you understand that you are agreeing to live together.

The actual words may vary in different cultures but the meaning remains the same, which is to stay committed and faithful to each other through the good and bad times, in happiness and sickness, for the rest of your lives, and so on.

An employee contract contains some important terms and conditions. The duties and responsibilities of the employee are clearly stated so that there is no confusion. The second aspect is the duration of the contract and the expectations of the parties involved. Finally, there are performance reviews to ensure that it is a mutually beneficial or rewarding relationship. If, at any point, either party is not happy then a remedial action has to be taken. They can make changes or renegotiate the terms.

In 2009, I met a couple at one of my seminars in London who wanted to start a business together but had too many problems. I tried to solve their issues but realized that, despite many attempts to resolve or remedy the situation, both parties remained dissatisfied. In such a situation, there is no option but to part ways or dissolve the agreement. This rule also applies to marriage. If at any point, one of the partners refuses to live up to the agreement or fails to fulfil his or her commitment or hold his or her end of the bargain, then, the agreement can be in danger unless both the parties agree to reconsider and renegotiate. Problems in a relationship can be fixed if both the parties agree to do so. If either party feels that what's broken cannot be fixed, then, the agreement is in jeopardy.

When a person breaks a contract by not keeping his or her end of the bargain, he or she has to bear the consequences. This usually involves loss of possessions as well as potential rewards. The person who failed to keep up might have to compensate the other party for any distress caused.

Similarly, if a person is fired without due notice, without a valid reason, or before the contract expires, he or she is entitled to additional compensation or severance pay from the employer. If an employee does not come up to the expectation of the employer, he or she can lose the job. This acts as a deterrent and prevents both parties from shirking responsibilities or not keeping to their part of the commitment.

If you want to get things done, produce results, or achieve success, then, along with any action or series of actions that you are willing to take, you need to create a commitment contract which will bind you to the necessary actions. A commitment contract is a written agreement that makes it mandatory for you to perform the said actions in order to achieve the desired result.

There are three factors to be considered when you make a commitment contract:

1. The first one is to define a goal, a target or a set of desired results. This has to be very clear, specific and unambiguously phrased.
2. The second one is to put something at stake that matters greatly to you. This could be something quantifiable or

measurable, whose loss you will deeply regret. Or, it could be something emotional and intangible like love, respect or friendship.

3. The third factor is to appoint a mentor who will review your performance and hold you responsible for your actions. You will give this person an actual piece of paper with the clauses of the 'commitment contract', specifying what you have committed yourself to achieving and what you are liable to lose if you fail to achieve it.

You realize and understand what you are doing here, don't you? When we make a commitment in our mind, we don't really articulate what we are committing to do or express how serious or important it is. When you make a commitment on paper, define what you are going to achieve and put something of value at stake, you are demonstrating your intention of sticking to your commitment.

The person you appoint will objectively review your performance, remind you to stick to your commitment and also act as a figure of authority. If you have tried to cultivate a new habit or give up an existing one and failed, use the commitment contract and you will see how it will immediately increase your chances of success.

Let's say, you make a commitment to meditate at 6 a.m. for ten minutes. Write it down on a piece of paper or type it and print it out. Make sure you are very specific and mention all the details of your commitment.

So, your commitment contract will read something like this: 'I will meditate for ten minutes every day at 6 a.m. I will sit in a quiet corner of my living room and close my eyes and remain in this position for ten minutes. I will set a reminder on my smartphone to open my eyes at 6.10 a.m. In case I am travelling or not at home, I will make arrangements to meditate wherever I am. Only if I am on a plane, in a bus or a car, will I be excused. I will perform this ritual daily for the next sixty days without any exception. If I fail to meditate even for one day, I will give up playing golf for a week. I agree to confess if I fail in my commitment. I will confess my failure to _____, who is my mentor, and he or she will decide whether I have failed to keep to my commitment.'

You can modify the words, but I guess you get the drift. Now, this is assuming that playing golf is an important part of your life, and you are willing to forfeit this privilege if you fail in your commitment.

You are probably wondering what if the person skips it on a particular day but keeps it to himself or herself and does not tell anyone about it. Well, commitments are made on the basis of trust, and we assume that eventually, your conscience will get the better of you if you don't confess to an act of omission.

For instance, an employee is expected to perform certain duties, but it is not possible for the employer to supervise each and every action. If he comes in late or goes home early, he has to inform someone. Similarly, if you are in a plane, 30,000 feet above the earth, on Monday at 6 a.m., then, you should inform your mentor.

When two people get divorced, it's not just because one of them confessed to cheating or one of them cheated and got caught. It is because cheating is a breach of the contract, and one of the two partners committed this mistake despite knowing the consequences.

Let's say you had a late night and failed to charge your phone. The alarm which was supposed to wake you up before 6 a.m. did not go off because your phone was not charged and you were unaware of this. These are special circumstances and taking into account that you had a late night and that your alarm did not go off, your mentor can use his or her discretion and allow you a concession. This is how a commitment contract works. It puts you in a position where you are less likely to take things for granted.

The next time you desperately want to achieve something, commit yourself to it by drawing up a commitment contract. You will see how everything becomes clearer in your mind and also how your actions are driven by a stronger determination to succeed.

When Commitments Create Conflict

When seedlings grow from seeds planted very close to each other, in a cluster in a garden patch, the gardener weeds out some of them so that the remaining get enough space to grow. The gardener replants the seedlings which he or she uprooted if there is space to spare. Otherwise, they are just discarded. The logic here is that if there isn't enough space between two seedlings, they won't grow into healthy plants or trees. Each of them needs space, nutrition, sunlight, water, and so on. Instead of letting all the seedlings suffer, you let some of them prosper and grow and sacrifice the others.

You might not realize it at the time of making commitments, but they demand a lot of time and effort. When you try to devote your attention to too many commitments, you might spread yourself too thin.

In such a situation, you will always be hard-pressed for time and in a rush, moving from one commitment to another. You will easily get overwhelmed and become stressed. This can lead to poor performance, and you won't be able to do justice to all of them. If you are feeling stressed, then, it's time to take stock and reconsider your commitments.

If you have watched a juggler in action, you will relate to the situation. When a juggler juggles with two balls, his movements appear smoother, effortless and even elegant. Then, when another ball is added, his movements become faster, and you can see the veins in his arms and neck sticking out from all the stress. The pressure to perform has increased. Add another ball or two and you can no longer see what's happening. Everything happens in a blur of movement. You know that he won't be able to keep it up for much longer, and there are high chances of his dropping the balls.

Do you recall the wheel of life? Consider every aspect in the wheel of life as a ball that you are juggling. Some balls bounce if you drop them. Some of them don't. Some might break because they are fragile.

Let's say, you concentrate too much on your career and finances and ignore your health and family. Your health suffers and your relationships grow weak. There might come a point when your health is beyond repair or your relationships break. This is you dropping the fragile balls.

Let's say, you take a year off to focus on your personal growth and learning. Then, you are ignoring your career prospects, drawing from your savings and depleting your financial reserves. If you make up your mind after a year to get a job and start earning, then, the balls which you had dropped—your career and finances—might bounce back. However, if you prolong your wanderings and squander your savings, you will go bankrupt. Some of the balls that usually bounce back can break if you drop them too many times. So, focus on all aspects of your life. Keep them balanced. Make commitments which you can happily fulfil without getting stressed. **Utilize my free 'Where Will You Be in Five Years' online course worth Rs 13,000, which will help you balance the different aspects of your life, on www.wherewillyoubein5years.com.**

Simplify Your Schedule

Make a list of your commitments. This is particularly easy when you have commitment contracts. After you have listed out all your commitments, prioritize them according to importance and the stage of life at which you are. At some point in your life, health may take precedence over career and, at others, family and friends may seem more important than personal growth. If you have doubts, seek a second opinion. Involve a mentor or well-wisher in whom you can confide to sort out your commitments.

After prioritizing your commitments, you will be able to decide if you can fulfil all of them or only a few. If you have too many commitment contracts and there is a conflict, then, it is necessary to renegotiate those commitments. You don't have to give up your commitments; you can defer them or postpone them for a later period.

Be very specific when you renegotiate your commitments. Remember that you committed because you believed that those goals were important. Now, at this very moment in your life, you may not have the time or the energy to do it but you can take up some of those commitments in a year's time, in three years or even after five years.

Reschedule those commitments for a later date. You can also delegate a few. Let's say you have been invited to a wedding. You RSVP, agreeing to attend. A few weeks later, one of your family members meets with an unfortunate accident, and you have to take care of him or her.

There is no question of your attending the wedding because you want to be there for your family. However, since you have already committed to it, you can request your spouse or sibling to attend the wedding in your place.

If you cannot delegate, then eliminate. There are some commitments that run the course of time and become a habit. Or sometimes, they lose importance and you no longer have to attend to them.

Perhaps, you no longer enjoy your weekly round of golf. You needed it at some point to network with clients or potential clients and also to entertain business contacts and keep them happy. Now that you have retired, you no longer look forward to it. However, you still play golf. Why? Do you do it out of compulsion or a sense of solidarity with your friends? If you stopped playing golf, would it adversely affect your life or would it free up time that you can gainfully spend on something else that is more important?

Are you wasting your time holding on to commitments that you made a long time ago? Time is finite. Time is limited. Time is short. We are usually told these things. However, how many of us actually understand the concept of time? You know you have twenty-four hours in a day and an uncertain number of years in your life. When you are young, you feel there's time for everything. As you grow older, you realize how limited time is.

Why does our perspective of time change depending on where we are, with whom we are or what we are doing? When we are busy, time flies. When we are bored, time seems to move at a snail's pace. In the next chapter, we will examine time and its relevance in our life as well as another quantifiable resource which is equally important.

11

Time and Money

'I have measured out my life with coffee spoons.'

— T.S. Eliot

Anand wants to impress his girlfriend. He takes her to one of the best restaurants in town, and confesses his love, 'I love you very much.'

She smiles on hearing this but doesn't seem satisfied with this declaration of love and asks, 'How much is very much?' He replies, 'As much as the clouds love the rain, as much as the wind loves to whistle, as much as bees love honey, that's how much I love you.'

'Oh! So, you are a poet, huh?' she asks. 'Do you love me enough to get me this diamond ring?' she says, and points at a jewellery advertisement in a magazine. Anand squints his eyes to read the fine print at the bottom of the page to discern the price—an amount including a few zeroes. His mind quickly tries to recall his bank balance and realizes that the amount he has in the bank exceeds the price quoted in the advertisement.

However, before he can say, 'I love you very dearly, and I will get you this diamond ring to prove it', reason prevails over emotion, and he asks himself, 'Is this some kind of a test? Does she really want me to buy her the diamond ring? Or is she just checking whether she can make me do anything?' He hesitates for a moment. Now, it doesn't matter what he says. That momentary hesitation has communicated to the girl all she wants to know about his love for her. She has already made up her mind to break up with him. Sometimes, it takes only a split second to reveal the value of someone or something. Sometimes, it takes a lifetime to recognize it.

Let's fast-forward to the present. The same couple is having a romantic dinner at a posh restaurant. Of course, they are no longer in their twenties but in their forties. That's right, around two decades have passed.

You are probably wondering that, if the girl had broken up with the boy, then, how did they end up together? That's a long story and we will not go into the details. The boy had hesitated to attach the value of a diamond ring to his love for her and the girl had left him for a while, but they got back together.

Every relationship has its ups and downs, and eventually the boy did get her the diamond ring. She said yes when he proposed, they got married and settled down. It's not very different from most love stories.

Let's come back to the present. Now, more than twenty years later, the man smiles at his wife and takes out a small package from his pocket and slides it across the table. Tara's eyes widen and her mouth drops open in surprise. Her eyes twinkle as she opens the box. It's a piece of expensive jewellery. To say she is happy would be an understatement. She is overjoyed. 'Happy anniversary,' he says. Twenty years ago, on this date, they had got married. She is speechless for a few moments but, once again, reason prevails over emotion.

'We can't afford this, can we?' says Tara. 'It's beautiful. I love it, but I can't accept it. You have to return it.' They have a discussion about their eldest daughter who is going to college next year, the swimming lessons that their younger son needs, the mortgage payments they have to make for their apartment, and so on.

Anand finally agrees to return it. He realizes that she is right. He doesn't need to give her a piece of jewellery to prove his love, not any more.

Tara knows how much he loves her, and he doesn't need to prove it. The same money can be used to pay a part of the mortgage or for their son's coaching classes or for their daughter's college fund. **You need to focus on your partner to sustain a successful relationship; you already know that, but how will you go about it? To learn more, check out my free online programme on www.wherewillyoubein5years.com.**

We value time and money differently as we grow older. When we are young, we have plenty of time but less money. As we grow older, we have money but no time. The truth is that money and time haven't changed, our perception has. It's important to value both and know the consequences if they are ignored. Time is especially important because, once lost, it cannot be generated again like money.

Compare Your Options before Taking a Decision

Our perception of time and money changes as years go by. Years ago, when I was younger, I tried my hand at many business ventures. At one point, I had two potential business offers on my desk. I had to choose between them. I could not take on both the offers, because I could not handle them together with the resources I had. One of the offers was from a client whom I knew very well. He was a tough negotiator, but he paid on time. He also guaranteed me a long-term contract. The other offer was from a new client. He offered me a deal that was far better than the market rate. The profit margins were better than the other offer. However, he was not ready to sign a contract for more than six months. He was being generous and my firm stood a chance of making more money in that short period of time but the client did not promise any long-term relationship or prospects.

I chose quicker and larger profits over long-term gain. However, the market dynamics changed within six months, and the client felt that he didn't require the services that my company offered. I had made decent profits, but I was back to square one, looking for new offers. If I had accepted the other offer, my company would have continued to grow steadily, if not quickly.

I am neither regretting nor questioning the business decision I made. Profits were a priority at that point, and I made an evaluation after comparing the profits I would get from both the offers.

Some things can be measured, quantified and compared. Other things can't be compared because they cannot be quantified. Time and money belong to the former category. Love, compassion, wisdom, sacrifice, pride and anger fall in the latter category.

Not Everything Has a Price

A few years ago, I attended a charity fundraiser. I met a business acquaintance and we started talking. At some point, the topic of the charity event came up. My acquaintance asked me whether I had made a donation. Now, I believe that the right hand doesn't need to know what the left hand is doing. I have always held the view that charity is something that you do discreetly and it is not something that you discuss or talk about. And here I was being asked point-blank about my contribution. I was a bit taken aback by the forthrightness of the question. I tried to change the topic but he persisted and asked, 'How much did you give? I was thinking of giving an x amount. Do you think it's too much? Or too little?'

I suddenly realized what was bothering him. He was trying to measure something that couldn't be measured. He was trying to justify his act of compassion. He was trying to quantify compassion by putting a figure on it. He wanted to make sure that his contribution was as big as mine or bigger. He felt that making a contribution was not enough, it had to be something significant. It was not the act of charity itself that mattered to him but the amount he wanted to contribute.

You can't put a price tag on these things. I tried once again to steer the conversation to a lighter topic. I asked him if he knew what was common between an accountant and a cynic. He gave me a strange look and asked whether it was a trick question. I replied, 'Both accountants and cynics know the price of everything, but they don't know the value of anything.' He walked away as if I had offended him in some way. Perhaps, he was an accountant. Perhaps, he realized he was a cynic. I am not sure which part had offended him.

Can You Buy Time?

We know the value of money because it can be quantified. What about time? Do we know its value? We can measure time in terms of minutes and hours or even seconds. For an athlete, even a fraction of a second is important because it takes only that much time to finish first or finish second. A patient who is terminally ill cherishes each day as compared to someone who thinks he/she will live forever.

Many people live their lives as if they are going to live forever. Our time is limited. It's like a book or a story or a movie. Whether the story is long, the book is fat, or the movie is short, eventually, they all come to an end. It's not the length of our lives that matters but the quality.

As you are aware, I conduct a lot of seminars and workshops in different parts of the world. The other day, I was checking my travel itinerary to plan my schedule. I noticed that it would take less time to travel from city A to city B than to travel from city B to city A. Basically, we would be travelling faster on the outward journey than on the return journey. It just did not make sense. I was curious and called my business manager to find the reason for the difference in the time taken. He replied that for the outward journey, we were on a non-stop flight, but on the return journey, we had a stopover. That explained the difference. But I don't like spending time at airports unless it is absolutely necessary. So, I asked him, 'Are there no non-stop flights available for the return journey?' He replied, 'Of course there are, but they are expensive.' I asked him why the non-stop flight from A to B was cheaper than the one from B to A. Apparently, it had to do something with the fare structure of the airline.

So, I asked, 'How much money are we saving?' He gave me a figure. I did a mental calculation. We would be spending more than eight hours at the airport during the stopover. I compared the value of eight hours of my time with the money we would save, and realized that it did not warrant the time I would spend at the airport.

Of course, I could have used my time productively even at the airport, but a lot of my work involves interacting with clients and business associates. I would miss appointments and meetings because I would be stuck in an airport lounge. I could make calls, write notes and even do conference calls, but I would not be able to interact personally with my staff or my clients.

This could be avoided by paying a little more money which would be less than the value of my contribution to my business. When I explained this to my business manager, he agreed and changed our travel plans accordingly.

What Is the Worth of Your Time?

I know a lot of people, especially those who work in companies, who have absolutely no clue about the worth of their time.

Try asking someone the hourly rate at which they would like to be paid? Most salaried people would not be able to quantify their hourly rate. They would say that they get paid an x amount of money per month. If you were a lawyer or an accountant or a consultant or even an entrepreneur, you would have an hourly rate or a quantifiable value attached to your working hours. You might have heard the joke about going out for lunch with a lawyer. Even if you pay for the lunch, the lawyer will still send you a bill for the time he spent with you.

In the industrial economy, when a worker was required to work over and above the stipulated eight hours in a day, he or she was entitled to what was known as overtime pay. This overtime pay was estimated to be more than the regular pay, if it were fairly calculated, according to the labour laws.

Why was the worker paid more for working overtime than what he usually earned? The logic behind this was that when a worker worked overtime, he or she was giving up their leisure time.

It is interesting to note how one's perception of time and value changes after one becomes aware of the hourly rate of one's time. How do you calculate your hourly value? If you are a salaried employee, divide your monthly salary by 160, and you will get an estimate of your hourly value. This is based on the assumption that a person works for about eight hours per day for five days a week. So, you multiply eight by five and then multiply the outcome by four (the weeks in a month) to get 160 working hours.

If you are an independent professional or a consultant or an entrepreneur, you need to estimate the money you earn and divide it by the number of working hours. However, your hourly rate and your hourly value may not be the same.

For instance, let's say you earn $60 per hour and your annual income is $30,000. Now, does that mean you work only for 500 hours a year? That would mean an average of forty hours a month, that is ten hours a week, which amounts to about two hours of work per weekday.

You could consider yourself lucky for having a lot of leisure time. On the other hand, you could also consider working for four hours a day and making more money. I am not advocating that you become a workaholic, nor am I asking you to work less. I am merely suggesting that it is important to understand the value of your time and find out whether you are using it productively.

Free Time Is Not Really Free

I am very particular about the leisure time I earn. I believe in family time, me time and also in work time. When I am working, I prefer to concentrate on work, and when I am enjoying myself, I don't like being bothered by work. It's important to compartmentalize one's work and one's life. It's what is known as work–life balance. To achieve the right balance between work and leisure, one needs to understand the value of one's time.

I am sure you have heard the phrase, 'being penny wise and pound foolish'. This means that we pay attention to small things but ignore the big picture, or we get mired in petty things and lose out on bigger opportunities.

Now extrapolate this theory to time. Do you focus more on the time that you spend each day on non-essentials and ignore how it adds up to a lifetime of lost opportunities?

Do you notice how, when you are working on something with a fixed deadline, you have a motivation to finish it within a stipulated time period? On the other hand, when you have no fixed deadline, you tend to prolong the work or even procrastinate doing it.

Let's take an example. It's the weekend, and you have no specific plans. You realize that you have been putting off revamping your lounge. You need to buy new furniture. You see an advertisement of a furniture company that has attractive offers. However, the furniture needs to be assembled and that would cost Rs 2000 extra. You decide to buy the furniture and assemble it yourself to save the extra cost. Just to save Rs 2000, you end up spending four times the time it would have taken the furniture company.

A few inferences can be drawn from this situation. You are a slow worker. Is it because you are not motivated enough? After all, nobody is paying you money to assemble the furniture. You might be saving Rs 2000 by doing it yourself, but aren't you wasting a lot of time, too?

The question isn't whether you can spend your time doing something more productive because it is the weekend and it is your leisure time. The question is whether choosing furniture and assembling it is the best way to use your leisure time.

When I read articles which tell you how to 'productively' use your 'free' time or leisure time, I wince. You have earned your free time by being productive, by working. Why should you spend it again on being productive? Isn't your leisure time meant to relax and take your mind off work?

When I see people on a holiday ticking off boxes, I feel sorry for them. The 'things to do' list which is an integral part of being productive is one of the biggest killjoys while on a holiday.

The travel industry and the obsession with social networking are partly to blame. Even on a holiday, we make a list of things to do which includes stuff like visiting all the tourist spots and taking pictures in front of monuments. Instead of enjoying these new places by focusing on the sites, we look at them through our camera lenses.

Why don't many museums or art galleries allow you to take pictures inside? They do it to prevent the paintings or the artefacts from being damaged and also to preserve an atmosphere of calm and quiet so that people can admire a painting or a work of art for its own sake and not because they want to post a picture of it on social networking websites.

Value Is a Variable Measure

There's more than one lesson in the above-mentioned stories about the value of money and time. When we think about money, we generally think about it in terms of numbers or units. You think about the money that you have in the bank or the value of the assets that you possess. So, your net worth as an individual includes your bank balance and the perceived value of your assets. The key word here is 'perceive'. As any financial adviser or accounting professional will tell you, money makes more money. That is, if you put your money in a bank, it will earn you interest. The percentage of the interest varies depending on the way you invest your money. The money you use to buy something of value can appreciate or depreciate over a period of time.

A house that you buy today could be worth ten times more in a few years or it could be worth less than what you had paid for it. How does a painting acquire value? It is the value that people attach to it. Even the painter or the creator can't put a figure to it. Factors such as how old the painting is or how much it has been appreciated decide its worth.

Similarly, the value of money is decided by the forces of world economy. That is why the value of gold varies. We think gold is very valuable. It is, because everyone has mutually agreed to use it as the standard for measuring value. However, gold as a metal does not have much practical use other than to make jewellery. You can't build bridges with gold. You use iron and steel for that. If you wanted to build an automobile or a ship, you would use iron. Does that mean that, for a shipbuilder or an engineer, iron and steel have more value than gold? No, it doesn't. Gold still has value because you can use it to buy a lot of iron and steel, whereas you will need a lot of iron and steel to buy some gold.

When you have money saved in your bank, you can afford to relax and spend more time doing things that don't necessarily involve work. That is why the rich have more leisure time. When you earn wealth, you also earn the freedom to use your time according to your wish. However, not everyone who is rich is aware of this freedom. Some people think that the only purpose of money is to make more money. If you are the president, the king or the queen or the finance minister of a country, you will have to choose at some point between keeping your treasury filled with gold or building infrastructures such as bridges, using iron and steel. If you choose to hang on to the gold in the treasury, then, you are delaying progress and growth by not building bridges. Hence, it is important to save and invest money but it is also important to spend it. If you don't spend it on enjoying your life, then, you are essentially not giving yourself the freedom to use your leisure time. In that sense, you are stuck inside a golden cage.

Time Is Money and Money Is Time

Money in the bank produces almost nothing, yet you can take the same money and invest it and its value changes. There is no doubt about the fact that time is money. On the other hand, money is time because, if you have enough money, you can do things you really want to. You can save money by putting it in a bank but you can't save time to use later by putting it away. You have to use time with caution. If you spend all your time in unproductive pursuits, you will end up paying for it and regretting it later in life. If you spend all your time in a rush, a few years later, you will wonder whether it had all been worth it.

Strike a balance. Spend money on things that matter. Save some of it for later. Spend time doing things that matter and with people who matter. Take care of your health, strengthen your relationships with family and friends, gain knowledge and grow wise. Acquire possessions or things that create an environment of joy, not clutter. Create freedom by recognizing the value of time and money instead of getting tied down to them.

Time has wings, they say. The link between time and money is undeniable. Time is money and money is time. You cannot separate the two. A busy man makes a lot of money, but he has no time. An idle man makes no money, but he is bored with the time he has.

The pace at which your money grows has to be better than the pace at which your time flows. Your time is precious. Don't waste it waiting around in airport lounges. Don't waste your money buying things that you don't need. Be a wise person who has both time and money and who knows how to use one to increase the value of the other.

Almost all the successful people with whom I have worked understand and value both time and money, and they also value the people around them. They know that these people form their support system.

12

Get Support

'Tell me and I forget, teach me and I may remember, involve me and I learn.'

— Benjamin Franklin

On a warm and sunny day, a banker was enjoying his holiday in a small fishing village. While strolling around the shore, he met a fisherman who was getting off his boat and bringing ashore the catch of the day.

'That's a lot of fish!' said the banker. The fisherman looked at the fish he had caught as if he were seeing it all for the first time, and then replied, 'Not really, there's a lot more fish than that in the ocean.'

'So, what are you going to do with all the fish?' asked the banker.

'Why! I'll keep some fish for me and my family to eat. The rest I will sell. You are not from around here, are you?' asked the fisherman.

'No, I am an investment banker and I live in the city. I am here on holiday. So, how long did it take you to catch all the fish?'

'Oh boy! You have a lot of questions. I don't know. Let me see,' said the fisherman. 'I went out to sea at dawn. So I guess, it took a couple of hours, perhaps three.'

The banker looked at his watch. It was hardly 9 a.m. 'So, are you going back to catch more fish later?'

'No, I am done with fishing for the day.'

'Then, what are you going to do for the rest of the day?'

The fisherman shrugged, 'I will go home to my family and see whether my wife has any chores for me. If not, I'll play with the children for a while. Then I'll go around and visit my friends. We'll probably have a cup of tea and talk. After lunch, in the afternoon, I will take a siesta. Then I will go out for a stroll with my wife in the evening. I may have a glass of wine or two before dinner. I think today is going to be a wonderful day.'

'You know what you should do? You should go back out there in your boat and catch some more fish,' said the banker.

'Why would I do that?' said the fisherman.

'If you catch more fish, you will make more money by selling it, right?' asked the banker.

'I make enough to fulfil the needs of my family. What would I do with more money?' asked the fisherman.

'You can buy more things and save the rest of the money. In just a few years, you can retire because you will be rich. Then you won't have to go fishing every day.'

'I love to go fishing every day. Why would I give it up?'

'What I mean is that, instead of working for just a few hours every day, if you work harder and longer, you will be able to make a lot of money which you can then put in a bank account. You can live off your savings and not work for a living. You can spend your days sitting around doing nothing or, perhaps, drinking if that's what you want to do.'

The fisherman thought about this for a while and then shook his head and said, 'Why would anyone want to sit around doing nothing? I would go fishing every day even if I had a lot of money. And why would I make a lot of money if I didn't need it? Why would I make money to put in a bank? What if they lost it?

There will always be fish in the ocean that I can catch and sell. I don't understand what you are saying.'

'What I am saying is that if you are smart like me, that's what you'll do.'

'Why don't you do it then?' asked the fisherman.

'What?'

'Catch a lot of fish, make money and put it in your bank?'

'But I don't know how to fish,' replied the banker.

'You just told me that you are smart. If you are smart, how come you don't know how to fish?'

There is more than one way to look at this story. One view can be that the fisherman is a simpleton who doesn't see beyond the immediate and, therefore, is not able to plan for a safe and secure future. You could also agree with the fisherman. After all, there is no guarantee that the money he puts in the bank will be absolutely safe and secure. Even a banker will agree that there are risks involved when it comes to investments.

The fisherman is familiar with the ocean and the rewards of fishing. He is not familiar with the world of investments and therefore is afraid of the risks involved. He is not aware of the potential rewards or returns he can gain. Is the banker giving the fisherman the right advice? In the banker's mind, he honestly thinks he is. After all, in the city, people start work at 9 a.m. or even later and work all day, till evening. To him, finishing the entire day's work in the morning seems foolish. The banker thinks that the fisherman is wasting his time by spending the rest of the day doing nothing productive when he can easily go back and catch more fish.

Why People Think the Way They Think

The point is that people have different opinions that have been formed based on the experiences they have had. Your thoughts and behaviour are influenced by the way other people around you think and behave. Your environment and community influence the way you think.

In some parts of the world, you have the right to own weapons such as guns to protect yourself, your family and your property. In other parts, it is illegal for civilians to own a gun.

In some places, you are not expected to tip or pay the waitstaff in a restaurant. In other places, it is customary to do so, and the waitstaff considers it rude if you don't. In some societies, it is polite to decline an invitation the first two times and accept it the third time. In others, declining an invitation means insulting a person.

Different societies and communities have different rules and customs. Similarly, people too have different views and beliefs as well as opinions. Your thoughts and beliefs are shaped by your parents and the environment in which you grow up. How they think and behave influences your behaviour. Teachers, friends and other people with whom you interact further mould and influence your mind and behaviour. What you eat, what you wear, which book you read, which sport you play, the language you speak, are all influenced by the community in which you grow up.

People's minds are conditioned in their early years, and what they learn then remains with them throughout their lives. People who are conditioned to eat vegetarian food from their childhood find it difficult to eat meat. **Understand how your**

mind is conditioned and ways to control your emotions to achieve the desired outcome. I have a video which can help you understand your mindset, as part of my free online course, 'Where Will You Be in Five Years', available on www.wherewillyoubein5years.com. People who are used to wearing shoes since they started walking are unable to walk around barefoot. Similarly, people in their late forties or fifties find it harder to learn swimming than those in their teens or twenties. People of one generation find the ideals of another generation different from theirs. When people talk about generation gap or culture shock, this is what they mean. People cannot agree on something because their mindsets have been influenced by the environment in which they grew up.

Connect with Like-minded People

If you come from a family of farmers, then, you are expected to continue the tradition and become a farmer. If a farmer's son aspires to be a doctor, it is important for his family to understand his dreams and support him. If his family doesn't support him, he has to seek and get support from other people who will understand and agree with what he wants. It could be a teacher or a friend.

It is pointless to blame others for not supporting you because they can't see things from your point of view. You can't expect the investment banker to understand the fisherman's way of thinking and the joy he finds in living a simple life. What is a perfect setting for the fisherman is weird and strange for the banker. The banker has grown up in a city and his thinking has been influenced by the media. He comes from a capitalist society where exploiting opportunities to create more wealth is considered a necessity or a measure of success.

The fisherman comes from a smaller, close-knit community where people know each other. He does not have many needs or desires because he is not influenced by consumer advertising or exposed to the new convenience products available in the market.

If you are planning to quit your job and become an entrepreneur, will you go to your current employer or boss and tell them about it? No, you won't because of the simple reason that your boss won't empathize with your aspirations to become an entrepreneur. Why? Because your decision to become an entrepreneur will affect your employer's business plans. Your decision will cause disruption which he or she would rather avoid than welcome.

Two competing athletes might become friends but they would never consider training under the same coach. They can be rivals in the field and friends off it. However, they can't afford to train together because it can potentially dilute the competitive edge that one seeks to have over the other.

When you are going to take a major step in a particular direction, getting the support of your friends and family is very important to achieve success. The support of a mentor, guide or other like-minded people can also help accelerate your progress.

Joining a dance or a yoga class might be a good idea if you want to lose weight, as you will meet other like-minded people who have similar goals or interests as you. It helps to interact with a support group if you are trying to quit smoking; you can learn from the experiences of others who have done what you want to do or are trying to do.

If you want to get into the hospitality industry, it makes sense to speak to someone who has worked with clients or someone who is currently employed in the industry. You can also learn a lot from reading a book, especially if you use the information to stimulate your thoughts.

Similarly, you can learn a lot from people who empathize with your dreams, desires and aspirations, or have gone down the same road that you are about to take. Like-minded people will have a positive impact on your life because they don't have anything to lose if you succeed. You will only invest in a business venture if you are convinced that it will succeed. If it does, you get the profits. If it doesn't, you suffer the losses. This might be a very cynical attitude to have but it is the reality.

Similarly, when you seek support—moral or professional— it is important that your views and beliefs match with those of the people who are extending their support. Otherwise, it will just be a relationship of convenience.

The relationship between you and a teacher or a philosopher, a mentor or a coach, is mutually rewarding. The people who extend their support are your allies. They may receive a fee or a share of your success, but they are involved in your efforts because they care.

Get an Accountability Partner

When you are putting plans into action, an accountability partner can give you the best support you need to succeed. An accountability partner is someone who has a stake in your success and stands to benefit if you succeed. If you are trying to get in shape or get physically fit, then, you can expect moral support and encouragement from a friend or a spouse. However, for professional support, you need to enlist the services of a health professional or fitness expert. If you are planning a career move or trying to get a promotion, then, you seek support from career counsellors, mentors within your organization, or you join a training programme where you will get the opportunity to interact with other like-minded people. If you have specific business objectives which involve market expansion or increased sales, support from a business coach or guidance from an adviser will bring you closer to your goal.

Your accountability partner will help you have clarity of vision. When you interact with someone who is involved as much as you are, you receive honest feedback. You don't want support from someone who is afraid to point out your mistake or someone who agrees with you all the time. You need someone who will question you, motivate you, inspire you and even take you to task if you falter. When you work out on your own in a gym, you set your own pace. When you work with others in a boot camp, you have to keep pace with the rest. Similarly, when you join a training programme or attend a business workshop, you are stimulated and motivated to perform. You know that you can be held accountable by a facilitator or a group of like-minded people.

Staying on the track which leads to success is easy. Performing on the track and achieving success requires support.

Reading a book will enhance your knowledge. Applying it will motivate and inspire you. Similarly, interacting with a supporter or mentor, someone who is engaged in your plan of action, will ensure that you stay committed to your goals.

Finding support for your cause or your efforts has never been easier. The Internet and social networking websites make it possible for people living in different geographical locations and even different time zones to interact.

The company you keep has a profound effect on your life. Notice how people with similar interests hang out together; how similar their problems are and how similar even their style of dressing is. Choose friends and partners wisely. You need to have genuine people around you who have the courage to call a spade a spade.

13

In Conclusion

'If I have seen further than others, it is by standing on the shoulders of giants.'

— Isaac Newton

The members of a large, extended family organized a reunion for a happy occasion. The family had invited people from different parts of the world; many cousins, nephews, nieces, uncles and aunts were meeting for the first time. The age-group of those attending spanned three to four generations.

The main event at the family reunion was a huge buffet lunch. All of them had gathered in the dining hall and were engaged in conversation, trying to catch up with what everyone else had been up to in the last few years. As lunch was being set up, the delicious aroma of the food wafted across the hall. This slowed the pace of the conversation.

'That smells good,' said a lady.

'Yes, and if the aroma of the food is anything to go by, then, I am sure it is going to be a very delicious meal,' said another family member.

Just then, they heard someone make a loud harrumphing sound. Everyone turned to look in the direction of the sound and discovered that it was an old gentleman. He was one of the oldest members of the family.

The old man appeared to have just woken up from a short nap. He was a big man with a thick moustache and beard, and a large nose through which he was sniffing at the air. Everyone assumed that he was inhaling the aroma of the food.

They soon realized that they were wrong. He was wrinkling his nose and making a face as if he smelt something unpleasant. 'There's a nasty smell in this room!' he announced loudly and looked around suspiciously at his relatives and asked them, 'Did any of you let off a stink bomb?'

Everyone sniggered when they realized what the old man was implying. They all sniffed and though they could not detect any bad odour, they were afraid to question the elder's authority. They started having doubts about the aroma of the food and even started questioning their own judgement. Someone said, 'Does the food really smell delicious?'

'There is a terrible smell,' repeated the old man. He had got up from his chair now and was walking around the room, sniffing the air. 'This whole room stinks. I am stepping out for some fresh air.'

As the old man left the room and the adults fidgeted uncomfortably, a group of children began to laugh uncontrollably. The grown-ups realized that the children had been up to some kind of mischief. They questioned the children.

First, they tried to cajole the children to find out what was going on. When this didn't seem to work, the adults threatened that the children would be grounded for a week and that brought out the truth.

The children confessed that they had found some smelly cheese in the kitchen which they had rubbed on the old man's moustache while he was sleeping. It was the cheese which the old man smelt when he woke up and that's why he had thought the whole room was stinking.

'It was just a joke,' the children said. Angry at first, the adults soon saw that it was a harmless joke and everyone laughed.

'The whole world stinks,' boomed the old man's voice as he came back into the room from a walk in the garden.

'It's the not the world, Grandpa,' said a little girl. 'It's your nose. There's a stink right under your nose.'

'What?!' thundered the old man. Some of the grown-ups led the old man to the bathroom and explained the mischief that the children had been up to while he was asleep. 'Wash your face and the smell will go away,' they explained.

Question Everything until Proven

When we are in our comfort zone, most of us behave like the old man. We see, smell, hear or feel what we are conditioned to according to our circumstances. The ability to look beyond the immediate is not always something we are able to do on our own. We need an external perspective, an objective opinion or an impartial or even blunt explanation to jolt us out of our sense of complacency.

At some point, we have to move out of our comfort zone and do things to produce results. When we are in school, we are conditioned to use textbooks to learn facts and theories but we are also taught to use our own judgement to test those theories. A theory is just an opinion or a view unless it is tested and proved.

There was a time when people thought that the earth was flat, that it was the centre of the universe, and that the sun circled it. This was considered a fact for thousands of years before someone questioned it, tested it and found out that it was a fallacy. The new theory that the earth was round itself faced much resistance until it was proved beyond doubt.

Knowledge and wisdom flourish when questions are asked. A healthy scepticism is better than being naive and subscribing to false beliefs. It is our fault if we simply take everything that is written in a book at face value. It is our responsibility to take every piece of information that we receive through any medium, be it from a book, or from a person, as something which needs to be analysed, tried and tested before we accept it.

Entrepreneurs and start-ups are familiar with the situation in which the old man was, where he thought that the whole world was stinking. When you break new ground, everything you do can be misunderstood or misinterpreted. The stink of rotting cheese right under the nose could be a very good metaphor for both success and failure.

You don't know what you don't know because you are not making any attempts to expand the horizon of your knowledge. As the old adage says, wise is the man who knows that he doesn't know everything.

Keep this in mind when you feel confident as well as when you are in despair. You don't know everything as yet. You don't know whether you will succeed or fail till you try. You will be in a position to try only when you have planned your moves and prepared for your performance.

Escape the Trap of Tunnel Vision

Did you know that the ubiquitous Post-it notes were the result of a failure? Today, it is one of the most successful products from the company that manufactures it. The yellow sticky pads which are a staple part of stationery in almost any office today, were the result of a failed experiment to manufacture a super-strong adhesive.

Spencer Silver, an employee of the company 3M, who was working on creating a super-strong adhesive for the aerospace industry was terribly disappointed with the results of his experiment: a very weak adhesive which could be used to stick two surfaces together very easily but the surfaces could just as easily be separated without leaving any residual stains on the non-adhesive surface.

Though Silver was disappointed with the failed results of his experiment, he had a lurking suspicion that there could be some other use for this weak adhesive. But, he was frustrated because he could not figure out a practical application for it.

It was another employee of the company, Geoff Nicholson, who came up with the idea of a bulletin board sprayed with the adhesive which could be used to stick notices or memos on it. This too did not prove to be to be a marketable product.

The actual idea of a Post-it note occurred to another employee, a chemical engineer named Art Fry. He was a member of a choir and always lost the markers or pieces of paper he used to mark the page he was singing or reading from in the hymn book.

In his desperation to use something sticky to mark the pages without damaging the book, he looked around and found the perfect application for the weak adhesive that Spencer Silver had created. To his joy, he discovered multiple advantages of using the sticky notes. Not only did the pieces of paper with the adhesive stay in place when he stuck them to the pages of a book, but the adhesive did not leave any stain. Besides, he could reuse the marker several times because the adhesive retained its sticky quality. That is how Post-it notes were born. The whole process from the invention of the weak adhesive to its application as a marketable product required the involvement of three people's inventive thinking over five years. It is, therefore, not easy to credit one person for the invention of the product.

Something which we think of as a failure could be potentially turned into a success. Similarly, companies and individuals can get complacent with their success and limit the extent to which they can perform and get comfortable within it. There is light at the end of a tunnel but in order to reach the light you need to get through the tunnel. When you are far from the light, you are virtually blind and grope around in the dark.

You can see only what you want to see. If you see the results of your efforts in the light of failure, then, you will believe that you have failed. If you want to get an objective view, you need another pair of eyes to look at the results and then, perhaps, you will be able to look beyond the limits of your tunnel vision.

Separate Illusions from Reality

When you look at the moon, do you see the shape of a rabbit or the face of a man? Do you discern meaningful shapes in the clouds in the sky, or a pattern in the wood grains on a table top?

This is just a trick of the mind or, more precisely, a quirk in our cognitive abilities. We know that the moon's surface does not look like a man's face or a rabbit. We know that if the clouds resemble a face, it is just our imagination and not real.

Similarly, when we are about to perform an act, there is always the anxiety that we may fail lurking in our subconscious. This fear or worry can very easily affect our performance. This worry stems from our awareness of our shortcomings or our limitations. When we see only the negative things possible, we can lose sight of our potential for success.

Sameer wanted to go to medical college but he could not afford the fees. He said to himself, 'I don't have the money to pay for college. Does that mean that I cannot go to college? No, it only means I need to find a way to fund my education.' So, Sameer considered his options. He could get a student loan from a bank or he could apply for a scholarship.

Sameer could try to get work in the administrative department of a hospital and request the hospital to sponsor his education. In return for the sponsorship, he could propose to the hospital that he would work for them for an x number of years after he graduated. What Sameer did was to identify the problem and then, explore the potential solutions. The ideal situation would be for him to save enough money to pay for his college education. However, this could take many years, and by that time it might be too late for him to get into college. Instead, Sameer explored potential trade-offs that would help him achieve his immediate goals.

Sometimes, it is important for us to go ahead and work with the resources we have on hand rather than wait for the conditions to become ideal or the situation to become perfect. Anyone can perform when they have all the advantages. Performing in the face of adversity is what defines a true winning spirit.

The Perfect Situation Doesn't Exist

Itzhak Perlman was struck with polio as a child but this did not deter him from becoming an accomplished violinist. Whenever Perlman plays at a concert, nobody notices his physical challenges because the audience is aware only of the music and his performance.

Perlman's journey to the stage before a performance is slow and painful to watch as he walks with the support of braces attached to his legs and crutches under his arms. However, pity is not the emotion that he evokes when he plays. The experience is a range of emotions that his violin, and not his physical condition, commands.

Once, during a performance, Perlman continued to perform even after one of the strings on his violin broke. He chose not to stall his performance when the string broke and wait until a replacement instrument could be arranged. Nor did he choose to cancel the performance. He continued to perform with a violin that was not perfect. It had a broken string but it was not beyond use.

Later, after the concert, when the applause had died down, he was asked what made him continue to perform despite the setback. He is reported to have replied, 'Sometimes it is the artist's task to find out how much music you can still make with what you have left.'

We often focus on the missing pieces when we know that what we should focus on is what we already have. Life isn't a jigsaw puzzle where you give up because a piece is missing. Most performances in life are not about having everything but about being able to do what you can with what you have.

There is no point in waiting for the perfect situation or the right time. The right time is now and the perfect situation is the one in which you are at this moment. Plan and prepare now, and you will be ready for the future when it arrives.